INTERNATIONAL
SPY
MUSEUM
HANDBOOK OF PRACTICAL SPYING

INTRODUCTION BY PETER EARNEST
TEXT BY JACK BARTH
ILLUSTRATIONS BY STEVEN GUARNACCIA

"There is nothing more deceptive than an obvious fact."

— SHERLOCK HOLMES

TABLE OF CONTENTS

I AM
NOT
WHO I SAY
I AM

I WAS
NEVER
HERE

INTRODUCTION

As a seasoned CIA case officer, I was wary when I was invited to write the introduction to *The Handbook of Practical Spying*. Not in fear of giving away trade secrets (espionage literary output grows daily), but in knowing full well that espionage is mastered, like baseball and poker, by doing it, not reading about it. Mastery of recruiting and handling covert sources is the core skill of human intelligence collection (HUMINT) in the clandestine service of the Central Intelligence Agency (CIA) where I served for over 35 years.

And just as in baseball and poker, there are "naturals" in clandestine operations, case officers who need virtually no formal training but have an instinct for operations and clandestine work. They hit the ground running the day they are assigned to a foreign post and step off the plane onto the tarmac. In real life, most of us don't fall into that category. We have to endure the formal training as well as the early years of trial-and-error maturing in the field.

For most, training can help, but living and working abroad, using a foreign language, and learning when to take risks provides the seasoning and maturity critical to a successful officer. Jack Barth's succinct treatise can't substitute for these, but in his light-hearted, tongue-in-cheek style, it does offer insights into the world of case officers and espionage and the multi-layered thinking so characteristic of its finest practitioners. Our instructive little manual will give the reader a leg up in gaining familiarity with the thinking behind spying.

What is a case officer or spymaster but a capable, well prepared, and sharply focused government version of a really crackerjack investigative reporter—one serving his country, however, rather than some newspaper's shareholders (James Bond, after all, was a British civil servant). Both are driven by an intense interest in the world and people and how and why things happen. Both fiercely protect their sources. And both hone their observation skills to achieve a degree of heightened awareness.

It is this "heightened awareness" that the book captures so well. Touching on many facets of the case officer's playbook from eluding surveillance to personality assessment, the book shows how the so-called "spy brain" reflects on situations and relationships in ways different from the casual, unthinking approach that most people bring to bear. In some ways, heightened awareness is an applied form of what Buddhists call "mindfulness," a constant and unwavering attentiveness to what you are doing and what is going on around you: Attentiveness to the max.

Former case officers and spymasters serve on our board of directors and as advisors at the International Spy Museum;

others visit our galleries waxing nostalgic over favored tools of the trade on display or a remembered incident, and some even volunteered items for this handbook. What was crystal clear, however, was that most had never lost their love of the game, spying in the field where it counts. *Mad Magazine* got it right: it often comes down to "Spy versus Spy." As much as anything, it's a battle of wits. Spy gadgets, tradecraft, and technology have their place, but in the end it's what's behind those "tools of the trade" that wins the day, what we call our "Spy Brain."

Today terrorism stalks the globe, eclipsing the CIA-Soviet KGB spy wars of the Cold War with a daily offering of bombings, bloodshed, hostage-taking, and fanaticism. Terrorism, too, uses the methods and tools of intelligence and espionage to advance its diverse agendas. And just as in the Cold War, nations and governments confronting terrorism will use those same methods and tools to deter and disrupt it. The basic principles of espionage and deception date at least from the writings of the legendary Chinese strategist General Sun Tzu who set down his reflections on warfare, including espionage and deception, some 2,500 years ago. What changes through the years are the practitioners and the technology. Even FBI turncoat Robert P. Hanssen, the counter-intelligence officer who succeeded in deceiving his country, his service, and even his wife, tried to coax his Russian spymasters into letting him use a personal data assistant (PDA) instead of risky dead drops in public parks in the last months he worked for them. They, wisely, wanted him to stay off the air.

A reflective person paging through our handbook might wonder whether he could possibly have any use for the trade-

THE MOSCOW RULES

1	Assume nothing.
2	Never go against your gut.
3	Everyone is potentially under opposition control.
4	Don't look back, you are never completely alone.
5	Go with the flow.
6	Vary your pattern and stay within your profile.
7	Lull them into a sense of complacency.
8	Don't harass the opposition.
9	Pick the time and place for action.
10	Keep your options open.

In East Berlin, Soviet intelligence had eyes and ears everywhere. To survive, Western spies had to follow "Moscow's rules"—go with the flow, stay within their profile, and assume they were always being watched. A friendly bartender might well be with the KGB or East German Stasi. Foreigners' phones were tapped. Agents shadowed suspects in cars and on foot. Everyone was a suspect.

craft of espionage. And if he did, he might question the ethics of such means. There is a longstanding principle in clandestine operations that you use the simplest and least intrusive means possible. Why recruit an agent to penetrate an opposition party to find out its platform and strategies if it regularly publishes its platform and its leaders brief the media on its strategies? Buy a newspaper and you'll learn all you need. The ethical issue is tougher.

In the world of John Le Carré, to take one popular writer on espionage, one intelligence service and its staff are pretty much like another—ruthless, amoral and faithless. I think he's wrong. That was not my experience. I think an intelligence service and its representatives are a reflection of the culture and values of the society in which it is rooted. The service, after all, is made up of the citizens of the country; they are not aliens from a remote planet. And so you, the reader, will govern your actions and the lessons you take from this book within the framework of your own ethics and norms. In that spirit, I encourage you to dip into this little manual and have fun learning, at least at one level, how to think like a spy.

PETER EARNEST

Executive Director of the International Spy Museum

CHAPTER

1

YOUR NEW SPY BRAIN

Ninety percent of spying is half mental, as Yogi Berra might have said. The mind is the only weapon that a spy is guaranteed to discharge on a daily basis. If you can adopt the principles described here, you may not be ready to single-handedly take down a super-villain, but you will be better prepared to counter the razor-sharp hats of hassle that the Odd Jobs of the world are continually flinging at you. The information in this book won't do you any good, of course, unless you can remember it, so start by clearing away that fluff in your memory banks. Spies have sharp memories, so why not you? That's the first step in thinking like a spy.

Yogi Berra wasn't a spy, but if he had been he wouldn't have been the first major league baseball catcher to adopt cloak and dagger. Besides donning the "tools of ignorance" for 16 pro seasons in the 1920s and '30s, Moe Berg racked up an illustrious intelligence career. During World War II, he was assigned to find out how close Germany was to building an atomic bomb. Moe Berg was a catcher who knew a few things besides balls and strikes.

● THINKING LIKE A SPY: THE TEN RULES

PREPARING TO BE AN ACTUAL SPY means developing mental and emotional strengths, not playing with a bunch of way-cool experimental gadgets and a tricked-up Aston Martin.

So how about looking at these mental techniques as if they were an attaché case full of wicked new contraptions, each there for you to put to use at the appropriate moment? There, *now* we're having some fun.

> **RULE 1: Act like you belong.** This is one instance where a spy rule actually works better for non-spies. Because no matter how low-key he is, a spy is far more likely to be questioned about his presence at some top-secret anthrax lab than you are after ducking into the lobby of a private office building to escape the pounding rain.
>
> So here's a tip for looking your most "I belong here:" Think of some smug person you really dislike. Perhaps Bruce Willis in a romantic comedy. Think of the face he makes that you hate the most. Now, "do" that face. That's it—that's the face that will grant you access anywhere you want to be.
>
> Don't lose your nerve. Like dogs and SMERSH (Soviet Army Counterintelligence, WWII) agents, officious busybodies can smell fear. Of course, if you are questioned and asked to leave, we recommend you do so politely rather than respond with a crisp karate chop to the neck.

THE TEN RULES

1	No matter where you are, act like you belong.
2	Behave purposefully. Especially if you have no purpose.
3	Blend in. Become a "gray man" or woman.
4	Develop assessment skills by practicing even in circumstances in which you are merely a bystander.
5	Learn to trust your instincts to make decisions—right or wrong, you will get better at it.
6	Never second-guess your decisions, but do analyze later.
7	Be aware that you may be overlooking things in your surroundings, especially if they are familiar to you.
8	Accept the fact that some level of deception is a necessary part of the job.
9	Don't be embarrassed to be suspicious of other people's intentions.
10	Upgrade your memory.

RULE 2. Behave purposefully. This simply means, don't stand around looking like you're waiting for something to happen. And don't keep checking your watch and sighing as if you're waiting to meet somebody who's late, because everybody knows that one.

Occupy yourself with a harmless activity: Some spies swear by carrying a book, which both gives them something to allay suspicion, and also passes the time for real. Dangerous trespassers and interlopers are unlikely to be toting around copies of *Ulysses*, or so goes the conventional wisdom.

RULE 3: Blend in. If you're downtown on a weekday, you'll want to be dressed as a smart businessperson. If you're in a dangerous part of town and it's late, better not to be. What you don't want to do is to be noticed. Keep your lock-pick

kit in your pocket.
And don't let your
nerves cause you
to chat away,
thinking you are
being breezy and

nonchalant like Chevy Chase in some Fletch movie; you
aren't—you're only drawing attention to yourself. Zip it.

RULE 4: Develop your assessment skills.

"Know your enemy," advised the ancient Chinese general
Sun Tzu in *The Art of War*. Like all predictive methods,
assessment is all about determining what future event is
most probable, based on everything you already know
about the factors involved. You can't always be right, but
if you can determine that one outcome is more likely than
all others, then act on that conclusion.

An experienced spy will know, for example, which train
compartment is safest to hide in when pursued by angry
border guards. Is it the one with the monocled colonel,
the Pomeranian-toting dowager, or the icy cool blonde?

So wherever you are, whatever you're doing, assess the
players and guess what will happen next, no matter how
trivial. A blind man needs help crossing a busy avenue.
Who will help him: the mouthy old lady, the goateed young
hipster, the nanny pushing a baby? Take a guess (assuming
you won't help the guy yourself). The more results you
witness, the larger your statistical sample, and the more
educated your next guess will be.

RULE 5: Learn to trust your instincts, and
RULE 6: Don't second-guess, but do analyze later.

Cultivating a spy brain basically entails using common sense. A spy applies her common sense in an instant, rather than mulling things over for a few days, making a decision, then wavering uncertainly, then choosing another option, then realizing months later that it was all wrong.

So if you're someone who dithers over every little decision, maybe it's time to step into a spy's shoes now and then. (Be careful of that heel—there's a homing device hidden inside.) Unlike the passive method described in Rule 4 for developing your assessment skills, these rules require you to take decisive action.

Ever heard the expression about acting on your first impulse? Well, that's true only if you have developed the experience for that impulse to be well-measured and intelligent. For example, if your first impulse upon hearing that your flight has been cancelled is to go and scream at a ticket agent, that's not good. If it's to first sort out an alternative flight, and then go and be unfailingly polite to the ticket agent in order to get what you want, that's better.

RULE 7: Be aware of your surroundings. We all think
we're aware of what's around us, but we're not, not really. Anybody listening to music with headphones or yammering in public on a cell phone, for example, is taking in almost nothing. Anybody who is benumbed from the routine of cruise-controlling through the same locale week after week is missing the details.

Although the most important reason to be aware is to anticipate potential danger, many other changes in our environs can affect our lives: transportation strikes, road construction, stores closing despite our having unexpired gift certificates there... Plus, in Chapter 2 we'll learn of a way to actually savor the finer points we might have overlooked.

RULE 8: Learn to live with deception. This suggestion isn't quite as odious as it sounds. What this means is that if you want to get along with other people, you have to learn how to express yourself with tact. For example, nobody who asks, "How do I look?" wants to hear anything but praise. Likewise, nobody who casually asks how you're doing really needs to know the finer points of your digestive system.

Many of the spy techniques in this book rely on deception, or at least the withholding of certain information.

> **"Our mission was spy versus counterspy, an intrigue-laden, real-life board game to which many of the contestants became addicted."**
>
> — STUART HERRINGTON, *Traitors Among Us*

SPYMASTER:
THE LEADER OF AN
INTELLIGENCE-GATHERING NETWORK,
AND AN AGENT
HANDLER EXTRAORDINAIRE

If you have a problem with that, you can hold your nose and get on with it, or you can decide that being a spy isn't for you. Go live on a deserted island. Like that guy in *Castaway*. Yeah, that looked like a *lot* of fun.

RULE 9: Embrace your suspicions. Nobody should live in constant fear, but it would be even worse to live in a fool's paradise, because that makes you a fool. So go with your suspicions—when the hairs on the back of your neck stand up, don't just scratch them.

A key principle to remember is that the people who make you feel the most guilty about being suspicious are the ones who are behaving the most suspiciously. For example, unfamiliar people who phone you or come to your front door have no right to object to the harshest of questioning or demands for identification. They are thrusting themselves uninvited into your life, and they'd better be ready to explain themselves to your satisfaction.

RULE 10: Improve your memory. If you can soak up the general spy principles in the first few chapters of this book, then see them put into action in the following chapters, you can train your mind to think like a spy—and that is a useful thing indeed, whether you're undercover in Tora Bora or just trying to remember what to get at the store.

● DOES THE CIA TRAIN RECRUITS TO THINK LIKE SPIES?

MANY CANDIDATES enter intelligence work straight out of college or the military, with minimal experience of real life. If they're going into, for example, operations work, they are assigned six to eight weeks of formal training at Camp Peary, the CIA's 9,000-acre spy school near Williamsburg, VA.

At Camp Peary, known as The Farm, classroom training includes such topics as How to Write Reports; What and How to Observe; How to Do Casings (reconnaissance); and How to Leave a Secret Communication for an Agent.

Away from The Farm, spy students, known as "career trainees," learn how to recruit agents by role playing with

Britain's domestic intelligence service, **MI-5**, suggests that new **MALE** applicants should ideally be no taller than 5' 11", and **FEMALES** no taller than 5' 8". "You should be able to **BLEND INTO** the background. We are looking for **AVERAGE** height, build, and appearance," the most recent application form states. (Under these guidelines, most of the actors who have played **JAMES BOND** would be **REJECTED.**)

other class members or retired officers. Training might involve being plunked down in a strange city for two or three days of simulated problem-solving. One trainee plays the part of a station chief, another the case officer, and a third an agent. If the agent's reports aren't very useful, the recruit has to analyze and address this problem.

Instructors inculcate recruits with the necessity of becoming first-rate observers and listeners, but that can't be taught in a classroom or in books. (Except this one maybe). Debriefing an agent is not unlike conducting an interview, and not everybody is a natural at grilling his neighbor. After eight weeks there's still a lot to learn. With the stakes so high, an intelligence officer straight out of spy school almost never is allowed to interact with real agents. A crucial first step is improving the recruit's memory.

● MEMORY

WHEN RUDYARD KIPLING'S KIM was training to be a spy, his mentor understood the primary importance of memory in espionage: He would drill Kim with the so-called Jewel Game. Kim would get one minute to study a tray of objects. His mentor would then cover the tray and ask Kim to give a detailed and accurate description of the objects. Predictably, as Kim got better and better at the Jewel Game, his overall memory improved as well.

Kipling also wrote *The Jungle Book,* about a bunch of singing animals; we have no spy-related lessons to extract from that at present.

● 10 REASONS WHY A SPY DEVELOPS A SUPERB MEMORY

1. Spies must retain an absolute minimum of written material both on their persons and in their homes and vehicles in case they are suddenly and unexpectedly taken into custody or their premises are breached by hostile operatives.

2. Often, there is no time to consult notes while in the middle of an operation. The briefing must be stored in the brain and be instantly retrievable.

3. The fictional identity of a spy under cover, or *legend,* must be absolutely ingrained in her mind.

4. A spy deals with experts in many different fields, and so must be a "quick study," able to absorb and discuss copious information about a variety of perhaps unfamiliar topics.

5. A spy might need to debrief an agent in certain situations—such as a noisy public space, a moving car, or a darkened street corner—where it is difficult to record the conversation or take notes, and so must be able to remember precisely all the salient facts.

6. A spy might be permitted a quick peek at the forbidden, and so must be able to recall in detail what she has seen.

7. A spy will meet many people, never knowing who might become important to an operation, and so must store names and background details—often based on a brief exchange—about many different contacts.

8. A spy needs to memorize in detail the geography of the area of operations, especially when conducting surveillance or countersurveillance.

9. Spies have even more passwords to remember than non-spies do.

10. A spy has to remember which switch is the rear-window defogger and which is the ejector seat.

IMPROVING MEMORY

Although some people have a photographic memory,
the majority of us can hold between five and nine
discrete pieces of information in short-term memory at
any given time. A common example of this is a phone
number. It's tricky but doable to remember one new
seven- or ten-digit number, but try to remember two
new numbers at the same time and the numbers get
all entangled.

Long-term memory is harder to quantify. Most of us
can eventually store at least a few important passwords,
PINs, phone numbers, birthdays, etc., because the need
to recall these recurs often enough to learn them by rote.
The process becomes trickier when trying to remember
crucial items, such as appointments, picking up
dry cleaning, expiring licenses and documents, or that
important phone message for your roommate.

Many people rely on appointment books, personal
organizers, and electronic appliances capable of storing
information, such as the phone numbers stored on the
SIM card of a cell phone. A spy might even use these,
but never to store crucial or sensitive information.
Not only would it leave this material open to possible
compromise, but it also allows for the possibility of utter
disaster when the notebook or device is lost or simply
elsewhere, its battery has gone flat, or it begins smoking
and emitting strange beeps. Is there anybody in the

modern world who hasn't lost a vital piece of information this way?

Although there are countless memory-improvement systems, or mnemonics, out there, almost all are based on principles of "encoding," or creating an association between what you want to remember and a vivid and easy-to-recall mental picture.

Encoding can help you remember individual bits of information, like a person's name or the combination to your gym locker, or it can help you commit to memory a long list in a precise order, such as the elements of the periodic table.

For example, let's say you've just met an intense artist with a monobrow named Frida Kahlo. To remember her name, you might say to yourself, "I wonder why she doesn't pluck her eyebrows—after all, she's *free to call out* for a pair of tweezers."

There are many commonly used tricks for encoding data, such as transposing difficult numbers into more digestible words or sentences. But perhaps the easiest way to create and later decipher encoding is to customize the system for your own personal passions and knowledge.

Peruse the following list, choose one that works for you (or invent your own), and try a bit of encoding: If you encode shrewdly, you'll find it's surprisingly easy to lock information into your brain for as long as you choose to keep it there.

5 TIPS FOR ENCODING USING NUMBERS

1. STREETS. If you are familiar with a city that has numbered streets, make an association between the number you want to remember and something along the street with that number. For example, if you want to remember the number 59, and you know New York City, think of the hansom carriages waiting on 59th Street just outside Central Park. (Perhaps you might even create a "sense memory" of the distinctive aroma of the horses.) If you want to remember the number 5914, think of a hansom carriage running amuck in Union Square (14th Street). If you want to remember 591478, think of a hansom carriage running amuck in Union Square while the driver eats a slice of pizza from that place you like on 78th Street. And so on.

2. INITIALS. Commonly, banks allow you to create your own four-digit PIN number. Convert the initials of a person you'll remember to the corresponding position in the alphabet, where A=1 and so on. For example, if you choose to think of Slumlord McGee, your parasitic landlord, every time you need to withdraw rent money, S=19 and M=13, so your PIN would be 1913.

3. RHYMES. Choose an evocative word that rhymes with each number, such as "gun" for "one," "glue" for "two," and so on. Then create sentences or mental images using each word in sequence. For example, 821 could be either

"I hate glue guns" or an image of a teenage wine-tasting where they "rate Blue Nun."

4. YEARS. Four-digit numbers can be associated with events that happened in the corresponding year. Obviously a number like 1066, 1492, or 1776 presents no problem, but even a number like 7791 can be a personalized combination, for example, of the year your favorite movie, *Saturday Night Fever,* came out, and the year your first child was born.

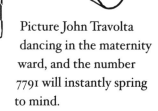

Picture John Travolta dancing in the maternity ward, and the number 7791 will instantly spring to mind.

5. TELEPHONE NUMBERS. Write out the phone number along with the 3 or 4 corresponding letters from the keypad. (For example, 2 = A, B or C.) The numbers 1 and 0 have no letters, so you need to call them "one" and "zero." If you're lucky, you can manage a word, or something resembling a word, out of some combination of corresponding letters. If not, you can create a sentence in which each word begins with a letter corresponding to the appropriate number. Obviously, this is a major time waster if you try to apply it your entire phone book—but thoughtful people will create words or sentences for their own numbers, and instead of telling you their phone numbers, they'll say something like the following: "My number? It's 202-393-7798. But you might just want to dial 'Washington-Eye-Spy-U.' "

5 TIPS FOR ENCODING USING WORDS, NAMES, AND CONCEPTS

1. GEOGRAPHIC ENCODING. Take a familiar route, one with distinct and memorable landmarks along the way—e.g., highway exits, street names, the rooms of your house, train or subway stops, or a daily walk. In your mind, move sequentially along the route, making associations along the way, perhaps creating a short scenario that takes place at that location.

2. ENCODE TO AN EXISTING GROUP. Begin with a list you already have committed to memory, such as the Presidents of the United States or your favorite musician's album releases. Encode each item you want to remember with a corresponding item on the list you already know.

3. CREATE ACRONYMS. Popular mnemonic acronyms include Roy G. Biv (the colors of the rainbow—Red, Orange, Yellow, etc.) and HOMES (the Great Lakes), but how about creating some of your own? For example, need to remember to phone Steve, Paula, and Yvonne today? Just think S-P-Y. (OK, it won't always be this easy.)

4. CREATE ACROSTIC SENTENCES. Using the initial letters of a list you need to remember, create a memorable sentence. For example, "Many very esteemed men just simply use naïve people." Figured it out? It's the planets of our solar system. Not to mention pungent social commentary.

5. NAMES. Think of a visual connection between the name and the person, ideally with the face. Or create a phrase that describes the person using homonyms—words that sound like other words—of the first and last name. If you want to remember a woman named, for instance, Diana Snowdon: Think of Diana Rigg from *The Avengers* wearing a hat that has been "snowed on."

REMEMBER!
THE ENEMY
IS LISTENING

A veteran of **WORLD WAR I**, Philip Johnston was the son of a missionary to the **NAVAJOS** and one of the few non-Navajos who spoke their language fluently. He saw that the Navajo language could be used as an **UNDECIPHERABLE CODE**, because Navajo is an unwritten language of extreme complexity. In 1942 he persuaded the U.S. Marines to try it. During **WORLD WAR II** over 400 Navajos enlisted as **"CODE TALKERS,"** using a language of coded Navajo words representing **ENGLISH LETTERS** that was **NEVER DECIPHERED** by the **JAPANESE** throughout the war.

NOTE TO SELF:
FIVE WAYS TO REMEMBER KEY INFORMATION WITHOUT RELYING ON YOUR MEMORY

Encoding probably seems like a lot of trouble at first glance — although once you've fashioned your own personal system, successive encodings become progressively easier. Still, if you are one of those people who become daunted at the first whiff of struggle, who would prefer to turn on the TV and veg rather than do something to make a lifelong improvement in the cognitive functioning of their brains . . . for you we present "Five Ways to Remember Key Information Without Relying on Your Memory." We hope you're happy.

1. Record conversations, lectures, meetings, or personal memos. (If you're going to record other people covertly, remember that this may be illegal in some states and some people might think this is not nice—that is, if they find out.) For the ultra-lazy, digital recordings can be uploaded to a computer, then transcribed automatically using voice-translation software. In which case the first sentence would read: "We could confer say shins leg cheers meaty soar . . ."

2. Take notes. In situations where this might be awkward, take a tip from *All the President's Men,* in which journalists Bob Woodward and Carl Bernstein would use the excuse of frequent trips to the bathroom in order to make notes in secrecy. If the "bathroom stratagem" is not an option, make notes immediately afterward—never trust yourself to remember something hours later, however brief the interruption. For just this reason, spies are instructed to write up their reports immediately after meeting with agents.

3. Place reminders in locations where you are bound to see them as a part of your routine. For many people, this is the screen of their computer or TV set. For a spy, this might be at the underwater entrance to an über-villain's lair. Or on the refrigerator. Using experimental, ultra-powerful CIA magnets. Or simple sticky notes.

4. Telephone yourself and leave a message. Hopefully, others will phone you as well, and this won't seem so sad.

5. Really, you should just start encoding. Sure, it might seem silly, even overkill to have to remember a sentence like "Ronald Reagan was in a red Rambler at a railroad crossing near Reno with (Sir) Ralph Richardson" when all you want to do is remember that you parked your car in row R, but which are you more likely to remember?

You never know what will happen when you leave your **SHOES** outside your hotel door. One diplomat's shoes were nabbed by the **KGB** while he slept, and a KGB-hired cobbler inserted a **MICROPHONE** and transmitter. With the magic shoes back in place, **KGB AGENTS** could **MONITOR** all of his **CONVERSATIONS**. Unlike Maxwell Smart's, the shoe did not have to be held up to an ear.

CHAPTER 2

ASSESSMENT

The human brain is often described as "the world's most sophisticated computer." But what if your computer started using only a small percentage of its processing capacity, overlooked huge chunks of stored data, and accepted input on a seemingly random basis? That describes exactly what most of us do every day. What we should do instead is convert our standard-issue gray matter into sleek, efficient spy thoughts. Because a spy is able to observe and assess in a way that normal people cannot.

Think of how many times a day you are forced to assess people, objects, places, and situations, and how a poor analysis costs you money and pain. A spy is exposed to exactly the same data from her surroundings as a regular person but perceives so much more that she inevitably chooses a more favorable course of action.

● HOW TO ASSESS PEOPLE YOU'VE JUST MET

ONE OF THE MOST FREQUENT complaints made by those who are forced to interact with society at large (or, as sociologists call it, "have a life") is that other people are always judging them. "Being judged" makes them feel paranoid, inadequate, or, in the case of arrested criminals, guilty as charged.

This rush to judgment is never going to go away, and frankly, there isn't much you can do about how people perceive you. So you better get out there and do some judging yourself. Whether motivated by tit-for-tat or by a genuine interest in people, when you start getting serious about assessing your fellow human beings you'll reap some real benefits.

In a sense, the world is one big flea market, where everybody is trying to sell you something, from friendship to flea powder. Now, when you literally buy a product from a reputable store, you don't have to worry about assessing each individual sales clerk, and the value of the product itself is evident. But in pretty much every other aspect of life, you need to make an assessment of the "seller."

Is this person:
- ❑ Who he or she purports to be?
- ❑ Honest?
- ❑ Dangerous?
- ❑ Offering fair value?
- ❑ A genuine friend?

❑ A possible romantic interest?
❑ Concerned for your welfare?

In the world of espionage, every player's interests fall into one of two categories: national or personal. A spy might ask if the person is:

    ❑ Who he or she purports to be?
    ❑ Honest?
    ❑ Dangerous?
    ❑ Offering fair value?

A spy shouldn't be looking for friends or romance on the job, and he knows the other party doesn't give a damn about his welfare. Beyond universal qualities, a spy must also assess individual preferences, goals, passions, and ideals. These assessments tell him which offers and persuasions might work best to gain cooperation. A spy asks:

- ❏ How can I best make contact with this person?
- ❏ What is the quality of information or access this person can provide?
- ❏ How can this person be persuaded to cooperate?
- ❏ If necessary, how can this person be compromised?

While a non-spy might hazard an assessment only when deemed necessary, a spy must be assessing around the clock. According to Peter Earnest, executive director of the International Spy Museum and a longtime CIA field operative, a good spy has to have a genuine curiosity about the world, how it works, and why people do the things they do.

Assessing people—developing a grasp of their makeup and personality—is critical for a spy. When a spy makes an assessment, she is looking for vulnerabilities—not in the sense of weaknesses, but rather as *points of access.*

Such assessments are always going to be less than perfect, because an intelligence officer cannot declare his purpose—unlike a psychiatrist, for example, who can say, "You're here for 50 minutes—tell me about yourself." The intelligence officer has to contrive to explore areas of interest, perhaps devising situations that will give him more information—situations to help him discover a target's potential vulnerabilities. For example, Director Earnest says he might "just happen" to stop in a jewelry shop while strolling with a new contact. This helps him gauge not only whether some shiny baubles might be one incentive needed to "turn" that contact, but also how interested that person is in luxury items in general.

You need to learn how to sharpen your assessments through research, observation, direct questioning, and analysis of body language. These skills can help you in everything from choosing schools and doctors to buying houses and cars, and in sizing up blind dates, partners, in-laws, nannies, your children's friends, divorce lawyers . . . all the way through life's journey, down the line to funeral directors.

● GETTING TO KNOW THE PLAYERS

CIA: Central Intelligence Agency, the primary U.S. foreign service for analysis, intelligence gathering, and covert action. Established in 1947 by President Truman as a continuation of the World War II-era OSS, or Office of Strategic Services.

NSA: National Security Agency, the far more clandestine U.S. foreign intelligence arm, formed in 1952 but not acknowledged until 1957. Specifically charged with SIGINT, or Signals Intelligence, including the interception and analysis—including code-breaking—of communications in any media.

FBI: Federal Bureau of Investigation, the counter-intelligence and security agency, and the law-enforcement arm of the U.S.

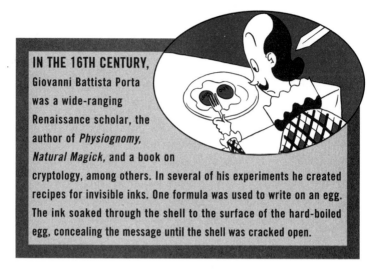

IN THE 16TH CENTURY, Giovanni Battista Porta was a wide-ranging Renaissance scholar, the author of *Physiognomy, Natural Magick,* and a book on cryptology, among others. In several of his experiments he created recipes for invisible inks. One formula was used to write on an egg. The ink soaked through the shell to the surface of the hard-boiled egg, concealing the message until the shell was cracked open.

AGENT: Contrary to popular usage, a government spy is not an agent. An agent is a non-professional, often a foreign national or an employee or associate of a foreign embassy, government, or military installation. Also known as an *asset,* although an asset can be non-human as well, such as a bug or telephone tap in place in an embassy.

FIELD OPERATIVE: Also known as *case officers,* these are spies who are stationed in foreign countries. One of their most important jobs is the recruiting and running of agents. They can also be known as *operations officers* or *field officers.*

SPECIAL AGENT: A great source of confusion, this is what the FBI calls its *staff officers,* although these officers are generally stationed within the United States. The assets they recruit are called *sources* or *informants.*

THE YOU-NESS OF YOU: A CLUE TO PERSONALITIES

DID YOU EVER WONDER how agents get recruited? In the case of the infamous Cambridge Spies, Soviet operatives looked for certain strengths and talents that would lend themselves to strong spy skills, among the students at England's Cambridge University in the 1930s. In many ways, it's just like a Hollywood director scouting talent for his latest movie. But in the case of the Soviets, they were also looking for weaknesses that they could exploit in a person, or ways to make that particular personality act the way they wanted him to act.

THE MYERS-BRIGGS PERSONALITY ASSESSMENT SYSTEM

The modern science of personality typing started with the work of pioneering Swiss psychoanalyst Carl Jung in the early 1920s. His personality types were expanded by Isabel Briggs Myers and her mother, Katharine Briggs, in the 1940s. They thought of it as a way to overcome differences between peoples, allowing for strength in diversity, and the ideas arose out of the carnage of World War I.

Although several recognized psychological tests for assessing and classifying different personalities are now used, the Myers-Briggs system is still one of the most popular, widely used in business and government. These systems are used to classify people, showing what traits and behavior we can expect based on these classifications.

With Myers-Briggs, all personalities are broken down four different ways:

1. CONSCIOUSNESS: Extraversion (E) vs. Introversion (I)

Interacting with the world outside oneself *versus* Being inside one's own mind

2. PERCEPTION: Sensing (S) vs. Intuition (N)

Processing incoming information at face value *versus* Generating abstract possibilities from incoming information

3. JUDGMENTS: Thinking (T) vs. Feeling (F)

Making consistent decisions in a rational, objective manner, based on prevailing norms *versus* Making ad hoc decisions in a subjective manner, based on one's personal value system

4. LIFE MANAGEMENT: Judging (J) vs. Perceiving (P)

Preferring things to be orderly, planned in advanced, and unchangeable *versus* Preferring things to be flexible, spontaneous, and open-ended

To evaluate your subjects, you think through each of the questions of a Myers-Briggs–based assessment test. (Several versions of this test, as well as an evaluation of the answers and different classification groups, are available online and in books, including Myers' own *Gifts Differing*.) Based on what you believe would be your subject's answers to these questions, you place them in either one category or another for each of the four classification groups.

Obviously it would be ideal for your subject to actually take a Myers-Briggs assessment test, but in this scenario we are assuming that you will be forced to tick the boxes yourself.

Each subject is described with a four-letter code corresponding to the four classification groups. There are 16 possible combinations of these traits (2 x 2 x 2 x 2). Long-term, large-group studies have yielded an extensive and generally quite accurate profile for each of those combinations. Thus, if you want to assess the character of someone, and perhaps tell how this person might react in a given situation, you would classify this person in each of the four categories, and then look up the established profile for that combination of letters. Think of it as the sensible person's version of astrology.

For example, someone who is very much a "what you see is what you get," straight-arrow type is probably an ESTJ (Extrovert, Sensing, Thinking, Judging). The profile for an ESTJ reckons they have cool, logical minds, are well-organized and good with money, scorn laziness, and prefer solid, wholesome products and meals.

But their characteristics are not all rosy. ESTJs are so busy living in the here and now that they tend not to see the big picture, and can run into difficulty due to poor anticipation skills. They also tend to short-circuit when forced to deal with the illogical, and can become impatient and lose their tempers when things aren't going their way.

So let's say you're a spy, trying to recruit someone you assess as an ESTJ. An initial thumbnail sketch could tell you a lot. For example, you would probably have poor luck appealing to the emotions of an ESTJ. You'd be best off trying to tempt him with the concrete

ENGLAND has had its share of **FAMOUS AUTHORS** who were also **SECRET AGENTS**. This tradition dates back to **CHRISTOPHER MARLOWE**, working for Britain's *first secret service* under Queen Elizabeth I. Other notable names are **DANIEL DEFOE**, who served as a spy in Scotland, and **W. SOMERSET MAUGHAM**, considered by some the inventor of the modern spy story. More modern writer-spies include **GRAHAM GREENE** and, of course, **IAN FLEMING**, the creator of **JAMES BOND**.

advantages of cooperation, such as specific offers of travel documents and transportation, or of money. Or, if a threat is called for, don't just glower menacingly—describe every gruesome detail.

On the surface, an ESTJ would seem to be an ideal profile for an agent. He follows instructions explicitly, delivers what he promises, and doesn't pursue his own agenda. However, an ESTJ might have trouble coping when anything out of the ordinary happens—a sudden change of plans, a missed contact, a hostile spy on their tail.

If you're trying to "turn" an opposite type, an INFP,

you might appeal to a personal code of ethics, or promise excitement and romance. But you should beware of recruiting INFP agents. They're flighty and unpredictable, they aren't the best at following directions…they can blow the entire operation, even get themselves arrested or killed.

Anthony Daulton Lee and Christopher Boyce, the young, real-life American wannabe agents were depicted in *The Falcon and the Snowman,* as confused, naïve and unstable. The KGB intelligence officers whom they approached at the Soviet Embassy in Mexico City assessed this instantly. So, the Soviets took what they could from them but kept them at arm's length. When Lee, a classic INFP, was eventually arrested just outside the embassy, this assessment proved prudent.

It's easy to see the value of Myers-Briggs-style assessments in everyday life. You may not want to classify everyone you meet with a four-letter code, but once the mindset takes hold, you will find that you know a lot more about people you meet than they may have meant to reveal. It is fascinating to take the test and find out if you are really who you think you are.

In Chapter 3 we'll look at some spy techniques for smoothing everyday interactions, but it all begins with assessment and analysis. This is why CIA trainers at The Farm spend valuable time teaching recruits how to fill out reports—putting their assessments into writing—when they could instead be demonstrating, for example, the latest version of the top-secret Fearless Robo-Monkey

● SPY TECHNIQUES TO BECOME TRULY OBSERVANT

BESIDES ASSESSING OTHER PEOPLE, a spy needs to assess her surroundings as well. In the spying game, you don't get the extra time to loll around that Bond gets, so you try not to ever miss a thing. Why do you need to be ultra-aware of your surroundings? Here's four good reasons:

- ❏ To protect yourself
- ❏ To avoid hassles and disruptions to your routine
- ❏ To increase satisfaction
- ❏ To get more out of life

The need to protect yourself is obvious. Nobody except a caterpillar lives in a cocoon, and even they have loads of predators. (Including birds, mice, ants, and stink bugs, in case you're wondering.) You may not need to be told this twice when you're in a strange, forbidding part of town, but the fact is, you spend most of your life in familiar surroundings. The odds are, if some stink bug's going to mess with you, it will happen somewhere known to you, while your guard is down.

You can avoid hassles and time delays by paying closer attention to the public services you rely upon. For example, if there's a change in your daily transportation—a strike, a detour, a service disruption—you can be parked in a traffic jam forever if you don't keep your eyes open.

You can also enhance your life by paying stricter attention to your surroundings. Is there anyone nearby who can fix a heel? Do you know of a hardware store near your office? You can try the Yellow Pages, or you can try this new thing they've got called *taking a look around you*.

In fact, as mundane as your regular routine may seem, it's guaranteed that there is an entire world that you are looking at with your bored, glazed eyes but not actually seeing.

HOW TO BE ULTRA-AWARE OF YOUR SURROUNDINGS

- ❑ Look for patterns amidst your everyday routine. Which neighbor picks up his paper at exactly the same time that you pull out of your driveway in the morning, and who walks the dog at midnight?
- ❑ Regard anything out of these ordinary patterns as possibly a danger or an intentional distraction.
- ❑ Focus on incongruous people, clothing, and behavior.
- ❑ Do not "tune out" familiar surroundings—look deeper for things you might have missed.

■■ LOOKING AND SEEKING: ■■ PROFESSOR JOHN STILGOE

Harvard University professor John Stilgoe teaches an aspect of spycraft by another name. He tutors his students in the appreciation of the finer points of the urban landscape, including highways, electrical grids, strip malls, and industrial parks. His goal is to make them hyper-observant of the more discreet elements of their everyday environment. His 1998 book, *Outside Lies Magic: Regaining History and Awareness in Everyday Places,* is a call for ultra-attentiveness.

Stilgoe believes that modern men and women are indoctrinated to ignore their environment: If something is mundane, there is nothing special about it, so it can be tuned out. Stilgoe believes that if we can dump this preconditioning, perceiving our surroundings with a child's eyes, we will experience rather than just inhabit the world around us, and notice things we didn't notice before.

Ever watch James Bond saving the world from certain destruction and get depressed, thinking, "I wish I was getting more out of life"? Well, there's actually quite a bit going on every day, all around us — we just need to start noticing.

● LIFE-AND-DEATH ASSESSMENT: KNOWING WHEN TO RETREAT

POSSIBLY THE MOST CRUCIAL part of assessment is realizing when it's time to get out of Dodge. The worst fate that can befall a prized asset is to be *burned* by the other side. Spying for the enemy is treason, subject to the harshest of penalties in most countries. A sense of decency, plus your intelligence service's need to maintain its reputation so it can recruit agents in the future, compels you as a spy to assess when it's time to shut down the operation and possibly even sneak out of the country.

Highly placed Polish officer Ryszard Kuklinski was one of the great American assets of the Cold War era. For an incredible nine years, he provided the West with over 40,000 pages of sensitive information, undermining the Soviet-controlled Polish military. And he did it not for money or kielbasa but for love of his country and his belief that Moscow had no right to be Poland's master.

Steady as a rock, he withstood a number of scares over the years and kept on delivering first-class intelligence. Finally, through no fault of Kuklinski's, the Poles became aware of a spy in their midst. Feeling the heat, and fearing not just for himself but also for his wife and two sons, he asked his American handlers at the CIA's Warsaw Station to secretly exfiltrate himself and his family from the country.

Kuklinski's assessment skills were clearly top-notch; otherwise he would never have been able to accomplish so much over such a long period without attracting suspicion. For this reason, the field operatives at Warsaw Station didn't hesitate in backing

NUGGET:
BRITISH TERM FOR THE BAIT
**MONEY, SEX,
POLITICAL ASYLUM,
OR CAREER OPPORTUNITY**
OFFERED TO A POTENTIAL DEFECTOR

his decision. With Polish intelligence tailing him doggedly, several attempts had to be aborted. Finally the Kuklinskis, hiding within a CIA vehicle, made it to Berlin, and from there to freedom.

Kuklinski had been such a productive and admired hero of the Cold War that it would have been a great tragedy for him to have fallen into the clutches of the Polish secret police. Particularly since Poland soon achieved independence, and would have debated whether Kuklinski's being a traitor to the Soviet Union actually made him a hero to Poland.

You may not have the KGB following you, but you have to be able to assess threats all the same. Who is that scary man lurking on your stoop, and what are you going to do to get around him and inside your building safely? When you know how to size up a situation, you can then begin to control it. Who knows? Maybe you'll become so aware of what's around you, you'll start assessing who is and who is not a spy.

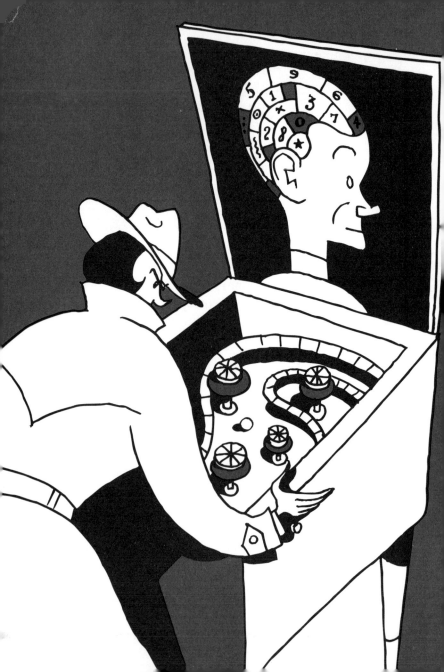

CHAPTER 3

MIND GAMES

HOW TO WIN PEOPLE AND INFLUENCE FRIENDS

You've begun to think like a spy. You have learned how to assess strangers. You're now ready to put that spy brain to work engaging with those strangers.

In the movies, espionage is all about fighting and outsmarting your enemies. In real life, spies spend far more time making friends. The best spies are the ones who can recruit other people to do the dirty work. And a good way to get strangers to risk their reputations, their liberty, and maybe even their lives is to get them to trust you.

Almost every business is a "people business," from editing *People* magazine to drilling spy apertures, although the latter is more of a "peephole business." You may not need your new friends to microfilm secret papers behind enemy lines, but you're not going to get hired or promoted or asked out by someone who doesn't deem you worthy. The basic principle of winning friends is to show a genuine interest in the other person. And that's something you just can't fake.

● INGRATIATE YOURSELF WITH STRANGERS

IN CHAPTER 2, WE TALKED about the importance of being able to assess other people. Now it's time to focus on how *they* assess *you*. Although spies operate in the shadows, they cannot afford to create any unnecessary enemies. You never know who is going to turn out to be useful or, more to the point, dangerous.

Let's say you're a field operative recruiting agents in a foreign country. Think about what you are doing. You're asking people to betray their country, to do things for which they could lose their reputations, their jobs, even be executed. The stakes are much greater than in everyday interactions, in which we may or may not succeed at making friends, but either way, nobody gets hanged if the encounter goes south.

The importance of trust in a spy-agent relationship is critical. If you can build a spy-agent level of relationship, you can build any relationship. In Chapter 5 we'll discuss spy techniques for forging relationships by portraying yourself as someone other than who you are. In this chapter we'll try to help you succeed as at least a reasonable facsimile of yourself.

> **" Tis the easiest thing in the world to hire people to betray their friends. "**
>
> — DANIEL DEFOE, *author,* Robinson Crusoe *and creator of England's first secret service*

11 TIPS FOR MAKING A NEW BEST FRIEND

1	Remain still and composed.
2	Smile genuinely.
3	Maintain as much eye contact as you can tolerate.
4	Employ the same body language you would use with an old friend.
5	Your opening statement is crucial.
6	Assess and then focus on the other person's interests.
7	Mirror body language and echo speech habits.
8	Plan in advance what you're going to say about yourself.
9	Be prepared for likely topics.
10	Maintain unshakeable confidence no matter what.
11	Work the silences.

● MAKING THEM REALLY, REALLY LIKE YOU

1. **REMAIN STILL.** Stillness projects calm and confidence. Fidgeting is not only off-putting, it also sends signals to even the body-language illiterate that you are being insincere, if not a downright twitchy freak.

2. **SMILE GENUINELY.** OK, some people are not natural smilers, so this might take some method acting. Think of Chris Rock gearing up to fight the forces of evil, and perhaps you can mentally transport yourself to a time when you sincerely felt like smiling.

3. **EYE CONTACT.** Most people are insecure, and so if anyone feels discomfort from this premature intimacy, most likely it will be the other person. Perhaps he thinks there is something wrong with *him:* spinach in the teeth, toupee-tape showing, etc. This puts him on the defensive—always a plus— and also allows you to sniff out potential weak spots (useful for later). Still, mustn't overdo it: think Bill Clinton, not Charles Manson.

4. **BODY LANGUAGE.** Just like forcing a genuine-ish smile, you can control your body language by play-acting that you are with a treasured old friend—though this should stop short of physical displays of affection and attempting to borrow money.

IN the 1964 James Bond movie *Goldfinger,* an ASTON MARTIN DB5 was equipped with machine guns, tire slashers, a bulletproof shield, oil jets, a dashboard radar screen, a license plate that rotated, and an ejector seat. Besides thrilling movie audiences, the car inspired INTELLIGENCE AGENCIES to incorporate similar features into vehicles used in places that were dangerous. It is believed that the Presidential limousine features gun ports, tear gas cannons, and layers of KEVLAR and other bulletproof materials under the car's sheet metal.

5. **OPENING STATEMENT.** Your first words are all the other person has to go on: Never box yourself in. For example, what happens if you say, "It's very smoky in here," and the other person wants to smoke? Likewise, avoid "Isn't it noisy/crowded/brightly lit" openers. Let him tell you what he thinks of the room. This gives you the opportunity to agree with them and make them think you have things in common.

There's no shame in starting with uncontroversial small talk. If you have a James Bondian wit, then by all means unleash it. The rest of us will continue to slowly grope our ways toward affinity.

6. ASSESS THEIR INTERESTS. Let the other person take the conversational lead. It's sad but true that if you prompt her to speak about herself, then just shut up and listen, you will be perceived as a great conversationalist and a stellar human being.

7. MIRROR AND ECHO. This is one of those magical techniques that seem completely unbelievable until you try them yourself. For example, if your subject says, "I know a lovely Italian restaurant; we had supper there yesterday," try to use the term "supper" yourself to let her know you are "her kind of person." If the subject has a habit of flicking back her hair, flick back your hair. (Sorry, baldies—you're out of luck on this one.) It's amazing to see the speed with which you can attain a comfort level with another person when you employ this technique.

8. TALK ABOUT YOURSELF. Most people will want to know what you do for a living. Although you should try to chat

MOLE: AN EMPLOYEE OF ONE INTELLIGENCE AGENCY WHO SECRETLY WORKS FOR ANOTHER

SPIES don't like to **AROUSE SUSPICION**. Because women used to be seen as helpless and weak, that provided perfect cover for female agents. **HARRIET TUBMAN**, known as "Black Moses" for rescuing three hundred slaves on the Underground Railroad, used her **MASTERY OF DISGUISES** to spy for the Union during the Civil War, as did **ELIZABETH VAN LEW**, the eccentric Richmond socialite. Van Lew brought baskets of food to Union **PRISONERS**, and emerged with the **NUMBERS AND DISPOSITIONS** of Confederate troops they had seen while on their way from the front. General Ulysses S. Grant later said, "You have sent me the most valuable information received from Richmond during the war."

only about the other person, you don't want to appear as if you're dodging the question. If you must talk about yourself, the keys are (1) You want to appear interesting without showing off, and (2) You want to allow room for follow-up discussion.

If you're a spy, you'd spout your cover story here, but for now let's focus on answering truthfully. If you are forthcoming, and include some inside dope on your business, most people will feel that they should offer the same level of information about themselves.

This enables you to re-focus on the other person and what she does. At that point, she'll probably forget that the discussion had actually been about you.

9. LIKELY TOPICS. If you're traveling in ultra-sophisticated circles, you'll need to hone your razor-sharp wit, but for

■■■■■ FOCUSING ON ■■■■■ A POTENTIAL AGENT'S INTERESTS

According to Peter Earnest, a former spymaster who ran agents for the CIA, one key principal of cultivating agents is to develop a genuine interest in their lives. "We always talk at each other or over each other, but how many people are genuinely interested in what your life is like?

"I got to know an individual, he had a great interest in American literature. I would often take him a book or something that was different. Never a big, valuable thing—always just a little thing. But it was indicative of my interest in his interests.

"A relationship developed. And in relationships there is often reciprocity. At some point he may do something that he realizes is very special for me. There may not be a particular time and place in which you actually articulate, 'Will you be an agent?' It may simply evolve over time."

the most part you'll want to calibrate your chat about one level above discussing the weather. Keep chatting about topical news: It's a useful way of finding out what the other person thinks. When talking about popular culture, you don't need to be an expert, but you should be able to name-drop well enough to keep the conversation going.

OVERCOMING PROBLEM ENCOUNTERS

Spies never accept a negative outcome—the consequences could be dire. Instead, they look for alternative ways to achieve their mission and are infinitely adaptable to the situation, and, of couse, always have a Plan B. You, on the other hand, might have to accept a knock-back now and then. But not before pushing a little harder first.

1. CONFIDENCE. Here's where you really need to think James Bond. If the other person doesn't seem interested in speaking to you, never allow feelings of inadequacy to creep in. This doesn't mean you should act smarmy or cocky or overbearing, but if you insist on wallowing in self-doubt, do it later amongst long-suffering friends.

2. SILENCES. Be aware of silences and how the subject reacts to them. If you are the cause of a conversational void because someone has asked an awkward question, turn the spotlight back on him. "Do you know, I'm not sure how I feel about that. How about yourself?" It's like basketball: if you have the ball, either shoot or pass it off. Don't just hold onto it.

● HOW TO TARGET AND MEET SOMEONE SPECIFIC

● ANYWHERE

You might want to meet somebody in particular, perhaps for business or because of some useful connection they might have, possibly for romance, or maybe they just fascinate you. Field operatives, on the other hand, basically want to meet and cultivate potential agents. When they target somebody who seems promising—maybe this person has access to certain materials and seems dissatisfied or otherwise approachable—they go through a few basic steps:

- ❏ They find out as much as they can about the person.
- ❏ They engineer a meeting.
- ❏ They insert themselves into that person's life.
- ❏ They develop a plausible pretext for a relationship.

Gathering information and engineering a meeting is straightforward. If you don't have an acquaintance in common with this person, you probably have an acquaintance once or twice removed. Field operatives call these intermediaries *access agents*. Or, if you know anything at all about this person, you can arrange to get close firsthand. For example, you can join a class this person attends, or dine at the same restaurant.

A spy will proactively create an access agent if none exists, or expressly devise a purpose for meeting. She might send a temporary employee into the target's office or arrange for another person to be introduced to the target by a mutual acquaintance. The spy herself may never actually meet the target — that way, the access agent is protected if the spy is exposed.

A spy will engineer a meeting by exploiting his status, or rather the status of his cover occupation. For instance, he might pose as a reporter, which not only gets him a meeting with the target, but also allows him to question the target with impunity. Or he might just pose as a lost tourist asking for directions.

BRUSH PASS:
A BRIEF ENCOUNTER WHERE SOMETHING
IS SURREPTITIOUSLY
PASSED BETWEEN A
CASE OFFICER AND AN AGENT

You might not want to go to such lengths. After all, when a spy reveals herself, the relationship becomes something else altogether—that is the design. But if you start a non-spy relationship based on deception, that relationship might very well end as soon as that deception is revealed—and you don't have that spy-agent thing called trust to keep it going.

IN A CROWDED ROOM

Spies aren't particularly known for using "party" as a verb, but now and then they do try to get out there and boogie—er, make contacts—at social occasions. Parties are excellent places to gather information, especially since a highball or two loosens tongues and inhibitions. Not all of us are party animals, however. Most of us have experienced the awkwardness of such events, and so maybe some spy tips can sand off the bumps.

WHEN YOU FIRST ENTER

GENERAL ASSESSMENT. Hang for a moment at the entrance and take in the scene: the layout of the room; the tenor of the crowd (age, dress, demeanor, loudness); whether many people already know others present; whether many people have been drinking.

MAKE A SUBTLE ENTRANCE, drawing no attention to yourself. You might let yourself get swept along with others, appearing to be one of a group. Once you're part of the throng . . .

TRY ACTING: Conjure up the feeling of a recent comfortable social gathering, like your Great Aunt Millie's 84th birthday party, or act like you are a character in a movie, with the world at your feet.

IN THE ROOM

STRIDE PURPOSEFULLY toward an imaginary goal on the opposite side.

MAKE EYE CONTACT as you advance, greeting anybody who returns the eye contact.

STOP AND CHAT when it feels right. It's OK to check out the room as you chat—that's the point of such occasions.

SEARCH for your target, but don't move toward the person straight away. It's OK to keep tabs on the person, however; you certainly don't want to lose the very reason you came.

GRAVITATE toward your target, chatting amiably with others along the way.

HOVER near your target, eavesdropping shamelessly and waiting for an opening. Then either insert yourself into the group by offering something to the ongoing conversation, or, if your subject is alone, move in for the kill.

● PUTTING OTHERS AT EASE IN STRESSFUL SITUATIONS

SPIES, WHO MUST DEAL on a regular basis with jittery agents, are adept at soothing the frazzled psyches of others. After all, it's truly a life-or-death situation when an agent's nerves threaten to blow his cover and hostile intelligence forces are monitoring every move.

Once the relationship between a field operative and an agent is established, it goes underground. Face-to-face meetings are limited, and spies start employing impersonal means of communication, such as dead drops and coded markings. This affords protection to the agent, who cannot be seen consorting with suspicious foreigners.

But the downside is that when you lose the human touch, the agent begins to feel isolated, and has nobody with whom to discuss her qualms and fears. It is important to arrange occasional, safe face-to-face meetings to reassure the agent, because, as in love, out of sight is out of mind.

The key to keeping agents on course is to convince them at the outset that what they're doing is worth it—the reward

> **"Every time the Russians throw an American in jail, the Committee throws an American in jail to get even."**
>
> — COMEDIAN MORT SAHL, *commenting on Sen. Joseph McCarthy's House Committee on Un-American Activities*

is worth the risk. Likewise, in everyday interactions, you must always consider things from the other party's point of view. Ask yourself, "If I were he, would I think this is a good deal?" If you're not sure, then it's probably not a good deal, and you shouldn't be surprised if it all blows up.

● REALLY GOOD SOCIAL SKILLS: THE CAMBRIDGE SPIES

THE POSH, DAPPER Cambridge Spies—Guy Burgess, Anthony Blunt, Donald Maclean, Kim Philby, and John Cairncross—were probably the most notorious and prolific spies ever to stroll the corridors of Western power. They met in the 1930s at Trinity College, part of England's elite Cambridge University, and went on to betray high-level British government secrets for over 50 years. Philby, who maintained his cover for almost 30 years, was so productive that he even ended up on a Russian postage stamp. (No, this is not how his cover was finally blown.) And although all were eventually exposed, none were ever prosecuted for their treasonous crimes against the state.

Back at Cambridge, the five were as privileged as could be, with glowing futures ahead of them. Indeed all rose into the higher echelons of British government and society. Blunt, as the keeper of the royal art collection, would ultimately receive a knighthood—the most embarrassing royal honor bestowed on any Brit until Phil Collins. Secretly, however, all were committed communists who felt they were doing the right thing in helping Russia to keep up with its capitalist rivals.

In the 1930s many people in Britain and America became involved with the Communist Party. But given the class consciousness solidly entrenched in the British system, it wouldn't have been possible for a young communist from a working-class background to have risen high enough to be of interest to the Soviet NKVD, which was the precursor to the KGB, the Soviet security agency. So the NKVD focused its efforts on recruiting the elite—a strategy that paid off big-time.

Over their years of treachery, the Cambridge Spies, particularly Philby, passed on information that affected some of the key events of the century, including:

- ❏ Allied military strategy during World War II, including news of the breaking of the Nazis' Enigma code and the development of the atomic bomb
- ❏ British and American intentions regarding the carving up of Berlin and Eastern Europe prior to the post-war Yalta talks with Stalin
- ❏ The West's attempted infiltration of spies into the Soviet Union during the Cold War, effectively sending these spies to their doom
- ❏ The FBI's breaking of Soviet codes (Venona), which among other revelations would soon lead to the Brits' unmasking of Maclean. This leak allowed Maclean to be exfiltrated from Britain before being arrested.

As damaging as the Cambridge group was to British and American interests, though, it's worth keeping two things in mind: (1) At least they didn't give away Allied secrets to the Nazis, and (2) While this was going on, American and British intelligence was collecting as much if not more juicy intelligence from Soviet traitors. It was all part of the give-and-take that makes up the overall game of spying.

■ ■ ■ ■ ■ FOCUSING ON ■ ■ ■ ■ ■
DALE CARNEGIE, MASTER SPYMASTER

DALE CARNEGIE was the granddaddy of today's self-help gurus. He was the first to realize that people would pay big money for someone to point out rather obvious truths about talking to other people. The funny thing is, those who study his methods overwhelmingly attest to their effectiveness.

Carnegie is best known for *How to Win Friends and Influence People,* which was first published in 1936 and still sells in record numbers. On one level, the book stresses honesty and sincerity in relations, but on another level Carnegie was one of the first of the self-help authors to put into writing the usefulness of the Machiavellian tactics of flattery and manipulation.

As with modern self-help books that stress unflappable self-determination, steeping oneself in Dale Carnegie's simple truths can turn a wimp into a spy-caliber player.

Carnegie's fundamental people principles are:
1. Don't criticize, condemn, or complain.
2. Give honest and sincere appreciation.
3. Arouse in the other person an eager want.

These rules could easily be outlining a three-step plan for a field operative recruiting an agent. The first two rules focus on winning friendship and loyalty, the third on "selling" that agent on betraying his country in exchange for whatever rewards the operative has dangled.

Carnegie also spelled out the rules of effective argument and negotiation. Once again the principles apply just as well for an American spy in Kiev attempting to turn a Ukranian military attaché as for a delicate potato-based negotiation between a supplier and wholesaler in Boise.

1. Begin in a friendly way.
2. Get the other person saying, "Yes, yes" immediately.
3. Let the other person do a great deal of the talking.
4. Show respect for the other person's opinions. Never say, "You're wrong."
5. If you are wrong, admit it quickly and emphatically.
6. Be sympathetic to the other person's ideas and desires.
7. Try honestly to see things from the other person's point of view.
8. Throw down a challenge.
9. Dramatize your ideas.
10. Appeal to the nobler motives.
11. Let the other person feel that the idea is his or hers.
12. The only way to get the best of an argument is to avoid it.

● MORE PLAYERS

ACCESS AGENT: Someone who has access to a target and could provide an introduction or useful information. Access agents must be protected just like regular agents, because it's usually not difficult to trace a spy connection once exposed.

AGENT OF INFLUENCE: Someone who can exert covert influence over foreign news media, officials, or pressure groups to further your objectives. We all use agents of influence in our everyday lives: "Did you tell her what a good guy I am? What did she say? Do you think she'd go out with me?"

AGENT PROVOCATEUR. An agent who instigates incriminating overt acts by individuals already under suspicion to help discredit them. Remember your bad boy schoolmate who spurred on one of his chums to write swear words on the blackboard while the teacher was just outside the door?

ANGEL. Surprisingly non-abusive slang used by intelligence officers and agents regarding members of opposing intelligence services—spying being one of the few professions in which participants show civility to their rivals. Right up until the moment they shoot each other.

CHAPTER 4

Q & A

GAINING INFORMATION THROUGH INQUIRY

Sometimes a spy learns all she needs to know by keen observation and assessment. Other times she'll need to elicit this information from someone—and that someone might be hostile.

Call it an inquiry, call it an interrogation: Regardless of the terminology, if someone is withholding vital knowledge, then you need to know how to extract it. Now, if you happen to own thumbscrews and a polygraph machine, and you have a private army of goons plus blanket global authorization for your actions, then you're all set, and you can skip this chapter. Otherwise, you will need a subtler approach.

"Social engineering" is a technique developed by hackers to persuade people to tell things they shouldn't. In this chapter you'll learn techniques for socially engineering friends, strangers, and loved ones, and for preventing others from socially engineering you. Just as important, you'll learn how to determine whether the information you've uncovered is reliable—because bad intelligence can leave you out in the cold.

HOW TO EXTRACT INFORMATION

SPIES GATHER INFORMATION; that's why the organizations they work for are called "intelligence agencies." But people in modern life spend a lot of time collecting "intel" as well—except for the time when they're watching professional wrestling on TV. Wouldn't you like to know what your boss and co-workers think of you? And if you are the boss, congratulations, but now intel becomes even more important. Are your employees performing their jobs properly? Are they stealing from the company? Are they working late and should they be promoted? And so on into every aspect of life. What records are being kept about you? What's the name of the person at your bank or credit card provider who is ultimately responsible for sorting out mistakes in your account? Are the shoes I want to buy going on sale at half-price next week?

Unless you live in some magical land where everybody is totally forthcoming with all the facts to service your every need—have you ever been to Holland?—you need to work on your capacity to probe. But let's not do anything as crass as asking questions: Let's do some *intelligence gathering*.

TIPS FOR SUCCESSFUL INQUIRIES

It happens to all of us. A bank, a finance company, a credit card issuer—anybody with the ability to damage your finances and credit rating—commits a clerical error with your account. Unofficial studies show that these "errors" favor the customer approximately zero percent of the time.

So now you need to straighten this out. You're at a disadvantage, because no matter how many commercials these organizations run in which they claim to be your partners, your friends, the assumption on their end is going to be that they are right and you are wrong. You are guilty until proven guilty—or until you give up in frustration.

Obstruction doesn't only occur when you're trying to alleviate a problem. Let's say you've heard a rumor about a job opening at a place you'd like to work. Or you're trying to track down a rare item for a birthday gift. Or you're trying to check someone's references, and the answers you're getting don't add up. In our paranoid, litigious society, it isn't natural for people to open up to strangers.

But all is not hopeless—not for those who can think like a spy. Because just as a good movie spy has no trouble kicking and shooting his way through the waves of faceless goons sent to slow his progress toward the super-villain, so will you have no trouble slicing through the institutional obstructions between you and customer satisfaction— if you master these proven spy techniques.

PREPARATION

While you're trolling online for names at the business you plan to approach, try to gain a basic grasp of company policy and industry lingo—very helpful in winning cooperation. If they start to perceive you as an informed fellow human rather than as some poor sucker who wants a job, any job, they might just help you get what you're after.

EXECUTION

1. TIME YOUR REQUEST. Choose a busy hour, if you're aware of one, when staff are flustered, or make your approach just before closing time, when they're watching the clock—either way, they're less likely to follow procedures to the letter.

2. INTRODUCE YOURSELF. You'll get more respect if you come on not like some beggar but like a busy and efficient individual making a reasonable and authorized inquiry.

3. DROP NAMES. Many organizations post information about their corporate structure on the internet or in brochures and other literature. Try to obtain a name of someone in the appropriate department. If you've ever asked somebody fielding your question for her name and then received what seemed like an improved level of service afterward, you'll understand the value of getting a name. This also helps get things back up to speed more quickly when you are inevitably disconnected.

4. BURY THE LEAD. If you require information that you expect might be withheld from you, be a good spy and ask other questions as well, in order to camouflage your true intentions.

5. COVER YOUR TRAIL. Continue to talk to the person after you have the info you want so that what just happened isn't so obvious.

HOW A SPY WOULD REASSURE A SOURCE

A spy is occasionally confronted with someone who wants to provide information, but doesn't want to be known as the source of the leak. According to one ex-spy, the best way to reassure possible informants is to talk them through the scenario that you'll use to assure that the leak will never be traced to them. It's not in a spy's long-term interest to burn a source, so ideally this scenario should be something that will actually be put into play.

HOW TO AVOID BEING AN INTELLIGENCE TARGET

ONE OF THE GREATEST computer hackers of all time, Kevin Mitnick, emerged from federal prison to become a high-profile advocate for the security of personal and corporate information. His basic mantra is that a clever person can obtain almost any information about somebody else, yet people and companies foolishly try to protect themselves by relying on technology and ignoring the human element.

Mitnick's 2002 book, *The Art of Deception,* details his considerable expertise at penetrating other people's secrets and tells how to prevent this from happening to you. These are a few of the sneaky methods to watch out for.

1. The Social Engineer (SE) plays for the long term, gradually accumulating layers of knowledge, so that when he's ready to strike, he's done so much groundwork that even the most security-conscious person will believe he is legit.

2. The SE might "groom" you with a few innocuous phone calls to lower your guard before moving in for the kill.

3. If the SE is pretending to be a staff member at your company, she will likely give herself a superior job title to yours in order to impress and intimidate you.

4. An SE might appeal to your vanity by saying she is a journalist or TV researcher. Certainly the glut of reality shows has shown that people will do anything to be on TV.

5. The SE will promiscuously name-drop other people at your company —but they won't be people you can consult at that precise moment. Sophisticated name-droppers invoke the names of assistants or even spouses.

6. The SE is well-armed with legitimate-sounding work-order, payroll, or employee numbers, not to mention the proper jargon for your workplace.

7. An SE might do you a "favor," such as warning you of a computer virus —he might have even sent you the virus himself. He'll then—surprise!—request a favor in return.

8. The SE might invent a problem, such as a manager who didn't receive a critical report, and then offer to solve it personally with a clever plan that will save your skin. This would, of course, involve your forwarding the report to the SE.

9. The SE might pose as a hapless victim, such as a new staff member or a stressed-out technician, in order to gain your sympathy and cooperation. Watch out for such lines as "My computer is down" or "I'm the new girl. I can't ask my supervisor again, she'll think I'm an idiot."

■ ■ ■ ■ ■ BREAKING ENIGMA ■ ■ ■ ■ ■

During World War II, the Germans had at their disposal the most unbreakable cipher machine in the world: Enigma. Enigma was a keyboard connected to a series of rotors by an electric current. The rotors transposed each keystroke many times, creating a scrambled, crack-proof outgoing message. This message was then sent to its intended recipient via Morse code. Enigma generated millions of combinations, and its elements were reset daily. To decipher a message, one needed to know that day's particular settings.

After being stymied for years, the Brits finally caught a break in May 1941 when they took a Nazi submarine. British sailors plundered the U-boat and discovered a codebook of naval code settings, printed in red ink designed to dissolve once wet. The codebook was taken to Bletchley Park, located between the English university towns of Oxford and Cambridge, where the Brits had already begun work on decrypting Enigma. Alan Turing, a mathematical genius, led a team of brilliant eccentrics in tearing away at the Enigma code.

Bit by bit they broke it down. It didn't happen all at once; rather, the boffins of Bletchley were able to steadily reduce decryption time to the point where the Allies could effectively act on the deciphered Nazi messages.

MAKING SHYNESS WORK IN YOUR FAVOR

CONSIDER THE COMPUTER HACKER—the stereo-typical social misfit. How is it that hackers are able to be so commanding and manipulative on the telephone that they're able to obtain password information from their reasonably intelligent, security-conscious victims?

It's because they are role-playing, and the best actors are by nature introverts. Extroverts want the world to see them as they are; introverts prefer to keep their true feelings private. Playing a role frees introverts to behave in a way that they would not naturally behave.

So, as you can see, you don't need to be a super-confident Smoothie McGee to play the roles required for spy techniques—in fact, your intro-verted disposition could work in your favor if you throw yourself enthusiastically into character.

● ASK THE EXPERT

JOHN SULLIVAN, retired CIA officer, served as a polygraph, or lie detector, expert with the CIA during the Vietnam War. He can extract information like a dentist pulls teeth, although his methods are usually milder. This is Mr. Sullivan's thumbnail guide to pulling information out of reluctant subjects. (Keep in mind that the bits about threats and interrogation are meant only in a professional context. Don't try this on the baby-sitter.)

ELICITING vs. INTERROGATING: In eliciting information, you learn the information they want to tell you. In an interrogation you try to get information they don't want to tell you.

ASK THEM QUESTIONS. If you don't believe them, ask more specific questions.

> **❝In wartime, truth is so precious that she should always be attended by a bodyguard of lies.❞**
>
> — WINSTON CHURCHILL

MAKE IT IN THEIR BEST INTEREST to provide information: either pay them or hold out some sort of carrot.

IF THAT DOESN'T WORK, try intimidating them with such threats as jail.

Here are a few questions we asked this master of the informational interview:

Is it possible to be a Human Lie Detector?

No. The polygraph measures heart rate, respiration, and electrical resistance. I couldn't do that by, for example, putting my hands on the subject's wrists.

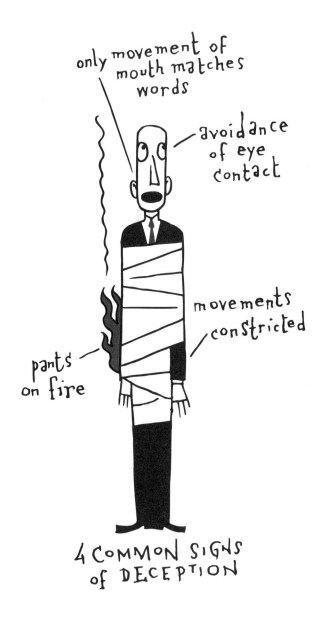

only movement of mouth matches words

avoidance of eye contact

movements constricted

pants on fire

4 COMMON SIGNS of DECEPTION

How would you grill your teenage daughter's new, alarmingly older, boyfriend?

I would try to engage him in conversation, ask what his interests are. I might not be able to immediately identify factual errors, but I would assess his behavior as he answers the questions. For example, if he says he was a track star in high school, I'd ask which event he ran. If he says the 440, I would ask, "What was your best time?" I know what the world record is, and could tell if he was lying. I would try to pin him down.

What is the best way to respond to hostile, invasive questioning? (I am not dating your daughter.)

Give short, one-word answers. Don't engage in a conversation; don't elaborate. Make your answers as brief as possible. If they keep pushing, just say you don't want to talk about that. Force them to bring it to you.

Or just say you don't recall. This goes all the way back to Watergate. John Dean became famous for saying, "I can't recall that." That is the perfect evasion. In Ronald Reagan's case—during the Iran-Contra investigation—it was easier to believe.

No one can prove that you can or can't remember something. You can say, "If you have evidence that says I did it, so be it—but I don't recall doing it." Depending on how sincerely you come across, that will determine whether or not you're believed.

CHAPTER

5

IMMACULATE DECEPTION
CREATING A COVER

Spies are always pretending to be anything but spies. If you think about it, this is an occupational necessity. Spies who publicly declare themselves are rarely invited by foreign dignitaries to come over and examine sensitive documents, for instance.

Most of us have no need to be deceptive 24-7, but at times things can go much more smoothly if you pretend to be someone you're not. The deception may be as simple as signing onto a website as MyFakeName@Bogus.com, or it may be as complicated as sneaking into Spinal Tap's hotel suite—although we must warn you that this latter purpose violates not only trespassing laws but also the space-time-reality continuum.

There are certain spy tricks to creating a believable cover: disguises you can wear, props you can carry, things you can say, lame fake names you can avoid... In this chapter our spy team shares this knowledge, so that you, too, can be not you.

● WHY YOU NEED A COVER

A COVER MIGHT BE a temporary identity, such as a more accomplished version of yourself when you're meeting your fiancé's parents for the first time, or a person who is above the legal drinking age tonight and has the fake ID to prove it. Or it can be a long-term façade, such as a "law school graduate" whose legal education consists of three grueling seasons of *Ally McBeal*.

Adopting a cover isn't always a good idea, especially when the purpose is illegal or locks you into a long-term lie, or when that cover is likely to be blown in a highly embarrassing fashion. However, adopting a cover can be a truly inspired way to attain some goals.

You can use a cover to reinvent yourself. Why spend a fortune on plastic surgery, 12-step therapy or lifestyle coaches when you can use spy techniques to be the person you've always wanted to be—even if it's only for a single party, job interview, bank-manager meeting, or day of luxury window-shopping?

You might want to adopt a cover to:

1. SIGN onto websites anonymously to maintain privacy and avoid spam.

2. GAIN entry to an exclusive nightclub, a screening, or to the VIP section of a club or restaurant.

3. BORROW (with permission) someone else's identity for the sake of convenience, such as making use of someone else's library card, gallery invitation, discount card or coupons, or video-store membership.

4. PUT your best possible self forward at a job interview—even if that self hasn't yet emerged in real life.

● WHAT BECOMES A LEGEND MOST?

GOING UNDER COVER is creative role-playing in the real world, in which most or all of the other players are unaware of your true identity. You will succeed in your cover only if you have thoroughly thought it through. You need to be perfectly solid with your legend; all of the elements, both material and mental, have to be in place.

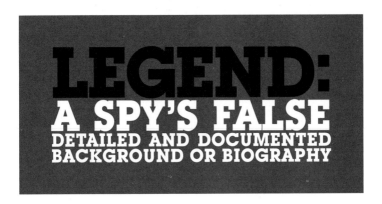

**LEGEND:
A SPY'S FALSE
DETAILED AND DOCUMENTED
BACKGROUND OR BIOGRAPHY**

POCKET LITTER:
ITEMS IN A SPY'S POCKET
—RECEIPTS, THEATER TICKETS, COINS, ETC—
THAT ADD AUTHENTICITY
TO HIS/HER COVER OR LEGEND

Your false persona doesn't have to share any of your actual personal attributes, but when you're first starting out you'll probably find that keeping closer to the truth helps you maintain consistency. Here's what you need to do:

- ❑ Develop your legend, or back story; you will need details for your fake biography, but begin with facts that are somehow related to your own life or someone else's that you know intimately.
- ❑ Decide on a current cover: name, job, and purpose.
- ❑ Choose an appropriate look or disguise.
- ❑ Gather pocket litter and other props. Each item must be appropriate to your invented persona. For example, impoverished students don't flash Amex black cards and wear Hermes scarves—not unless they are being portrayed in a movie by Jerry Lewis.

Consistency might be the most difficult aspect of going under cover. You can have a sensational disguise, but if you're supposed to work at the Zippy Mart and you come calling in a Lexus, you are probably not going to convince most folks. That's why researching your legend first is so important. Here are a few tips in finding out who you really aren't:

1. STUDY TRAVEL GUIDES and message boards from your supposed hometown. If someone you meet should also happen to come from your pretend hometown, explain that you left there at an early age, and then shift the conversation to more familiar ground.

2. LEARN LOCAL CUSTOMS, ACCENTS, AND LINGO. You
don't want to be quirky and different; it's tough enough
to pass muster by being nondescript.

3. VOCABULARY AND EDUCATION. Match your vocabulary
to your new identity. Know exactly how much education
your character has had, and whether he or she would use
certain words or flaunt any fancy book learnin'.

● FIVE TIPS FOR MAINTAINING CONSISTENCY

1. Use the correct jargon for your profession. Even the
most original thinkers are guilty of falling into the speech
patterns of their peers.

2. Know how much travel experience your character has
had. Vacations are a popular conversation topic; if you
don't know the difference between the Bois de Boulogne
and the Tuileries, don't bring up Paris.

3. Avoid personal discussions about your pretend family.
Even if you have a solid grip on your family legend, all
family stories get complicated, and you can trip up. If
you claim to have a partner or kids, people will naturally
wonder where they are.

4. Try to close intense grilling sessions quickly, but to the
other party's satisfaction. The trick is to answer questions

COVER: THE OSTENSIBLE OCCUPATION OF AN INTELLIGENCE AGENT; MUST BE CONSISTENT WITH THE SUBJECT'S BACKGROUND AND PRESENCE IN **TARGET AREA**

before they are asked, so that you control the level of information. For example, if you say, "I am a professional athlete," the other party might ask your sport, your team, your position, where you attended college, etc. But if you say, "I play jai alai in Miami. I used to play in Bridgeport, Connecticut, but because of all the other attractive Native American-based gambling options around there, we got closed down," you might save yourself a lot of nosy questions.

5. If you think you're about to be exposed, escape the one-on-one situation by inviting another person to join your conversation, or by using body language to expand the discussion circle. This diverts attention onto the new person, giving you time to get back into character and compose yourself.

■■■■■ FALSE FLAGS ■■■■■

One of the niftiest tricks in spying is to convince a prospect whom you know wouldn't want to work on your country's behalf that she will be spying for a different country—a country she favors. If a clever field operative recruits an agent under such a misapprehension, that deluded agent is said to be working under a false flag.

Another way to use a false flag is to pretend to be a spy from an enemy intelligence service trying to recruit a member of your own service. This is more likely to be employed against a spy who is already under suspicion of being a mole, rather than as a random stab at entrapment.

This is exactly what happened in 1995, when Earl Edwin Pitts, a veteran FBI agent, was fingered by an informer as a turncoat who had been supplying the KGB (and later its successor, the SVRR) with everything he knew of his sensitive, highly classified operations. To confirm Pitts's betrayal and ascertain how much he had given away, FBI agents posed as SVRR operatives and approached him. Pitts readily gave them anything he could lay his mitts on. Pitts was arrested in 1996, and pleaded guilty to two counts of espionage. He was sentenced to 27 years in prison.

DISGUISE

ONCE YOU'RE SERIOUS about going under cover, the next logical step is to incorporate a disguise. You may use it just as a way of "getting into" your adopted character, you may need to deceive certain people who already know you, or you may have to look like two different people in a single location.

The CIA has long taken this aspect of spycraft very seriously. The Company has even consulted makeup and special effects

DEEP COVER:
AN ELABORATE FALSE IDENTITY, ESTABLISHED BY
LIVING AND WORKING
IN A FOREIGN COUNTRY FOR YEARS
BEFORE INITIATING
ESPIONAGE ACTIVITIES

experts from Hollywood to develop disguises for its spies. In fact, Hollywood makeup artist John Chambers was secretly awarded the CIA Intelligence Medal of Merit in the early 1980s.

During the 1980 Iran hostage crisis, CIA disguise specialist Antonio Mendez helped six American diplomats escape the country by disguising them as a Canadian film crew scouting movie locations. The consul general was transformed into a flamboyant film director in tight pants, gold chains, and a pompadour.

● A SPY'S DISGUISE DISCLOSURES

JACK PLATT was a CIA master of "denied-area operations"—entering countries where he was not permitted. He also trained other spies to operate in hostile environments. In an interview he discussed using disguises to get in—and out—of denied areas without harm:

"I might go into a building and once inside I'd change my identity, do an 'identity transfer.' In denied-area operations,

I need to disappear for about 45 minutes. Any longer, and they'll start to wonder where I am.

"I'd carry the same beat-up bag all the time, so they're used to seeing me with it. It needs to be a briefcase or a backpack, because it has to be large enough to hold shoes and other things. It might also hold a shirt, and a different-colored pair of trousers. Levis are good, because they're worn all over the world, even back during the Cold War.

"I always bring a change of shoes. Good surveillance doesn't look at your coat or your trousers— they know it's easy to change those. But rarely will someone change their shoes."

It's slightly more work if the people you'll be encountering know who you are.

"We can all recognize people we know from about 50 yards off. You can't see the face, but you know the way the torso looks, the way he walks. First thing I would do is put a marble in one shoe—man, am I going to walk different. I'll be the guy with the limp. And then when I take the marble out, 'the guy with the limp' has disappeared forever."

CELEBRITY SPIES

WE'LL PROBABLY NEVER KNOW all the famous people who have worked for their countries as spies over the years. That's the nature of spying. But a surprising number are known to us, even if it's not always clear exactly what they did.

Celebrity is the ultimate cover. Not only are celebrities allowed access to places where the general public is not, but most people are so awed by fame that they drop their guard around celebrities and become fawning fans. Plus, even if you catch them in the act of espionage, it's a potential PR nightmare to execute them.

World War II attracted all types of celebrities. John Wayne's favorite director, John Ford, pitched in for the Office of Strategic Services (OSS), along with actor Sterling Hayden, who would later become best-known as the crazed general

Jack D. Ripper in *Dr. Strangelove*. Before gaining fame as one of the first TV chefs, Julia Child worked in the OSS, processing classified documents for the Americans in Ceylon. The Berlin-born expat movie star Marlene Dietrich recorded pop songs for the OSS that were broadcast to German soldiers as American propaganda. Cary Grant worked for British Intelligence during the war, as did (reputedly) the writers Noel Coward and Patrick O'Brian.

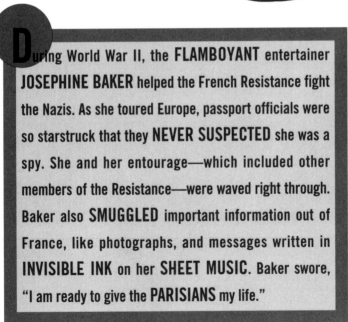

During World War II, the **FLAMBOYANT** entertainer **JOSEPHINE BAKER** helped the French Resistance fight the Nazis. As she toured Europe, passport officials were so starstruck that they **NEVER SUSPECTED** she was a spy. She and her entourage—which included other members of the Resistance—were waved right through. Baker also **SMUGGLED** important information out of France, like photographs, and messages written in **INVISIBLE INK** on her **SHEET MUSIC**. Baker swore, "I am ready to give the **PARISIANS** my life."

6

KILLING MOSQUITOS WITH A CANNON

USING SPY TECHNIQUES TO DEAL WITH EVERYDAY PROBLEMS

So far you've learned to observe, assess, remember, befriend, question and deceive. Now it's time to put all of these skills together to "grease the wheels" of everyday life. How many times have you said, "I bet if I were a trained spy—or at least trained to be a spy via the pages of a highly entertaining book— this wouldn't be a problem"? Well, in this chapter we'll help you make that peculiar supposition a reality.

For example, ever hear the expression "Hide in plain sight"? Well, sometimes it's better to hide things in a more *hidden* sort of way. Hiding behavior can improve your life in large respects like protecting your so-called privacy or in smaller details like infallibly squirreling away your house keys—a spy technique known as the dead drop.

Spies are also expert at entering forbidden places, and you should be too. So many of the good things in life are unreasonably denied to us, like exclusive nightclubs and other people's conversations... It's time to take your inner spy out for a walk.

> **❝There is nowhere you cannot put spies to good use.❞**
> — SUN TZU, *the Art of War*

● INFILTRATING

IN THE CLASSIC SPY MOVIE SCENARIO the hero cleverly infiltrates the belly of the beast, learns details of the nefarious plan, unravels the plan, destroys the complex of evil while perhaps rescuing a comely hostage, and then escapes (barely). In real life, you might have occasion to do some infiltration of your own—though probably on a smaller scale.

Here are several scenarios:

- ❑ You're "caught short" in public. The nearest bathroom is "for customers only," but you aren't a customer.
- ❑ The last tickets have just been sold to the Peter, Paul, and Mary reunion concert. You want in.
- ❑ You're doing research and need access to a denied area, such as a special section of a library or a museum.
- ❑ You want to enter an exclusive nightclub.
- ❑ Not satisfied with entering that nightclub, now you want to enter the VIP section, perhaps because the president of France is there and you wish to discuss cheese.

A CONVERSATION ON INFILTRATION

Security has tightened at most places since 9/11. You don't want to mess with these people, so the answer is not confrontation but stealth. You want to fly under their radar, not bounce against their armor.

We asked former CIA spymasters Peter Earnest and Jack Platt to explain how they would go about infiltrating everyday locations.

Peter Earnest: If you want to infiltrate anywhere, first learn how the people who belong there dress and comport themselves, then try to come as close to that as you can. It's not for nothing that the phrase "little gray man" is used in describing spies. The one thing you're trying not to do is attract attention.

Security officers are conditioned to react to certain appearances in certain ways. If you don't set off those alarm bells, you can pretend to be meeting somebody, you can pretend that you were there earlier and you left

DENIED-AREA OPERATIONS:
SPYING IN AREAS
WHERE THERE IS EXTREME AND
HOSTILE SURVEILLANCE

something, or you can just stride right in. I always carry reading material to appear casual and nonchalant—plus, to have something to read. It's also a way to signal a stranger you're meeting: "I'll be carrying a copy of *Time* and wearing a yellow scarf." Once you appear to be reading something, people mentally discount you. Reading is a purposeful act—the issue when you're trying to blend in is to look purposeful. It's when you don't look purposeful—when you're looking around— that you draw attention. When you walk into the building, you are going somewhere. The more you do the expected, the more comfortable the people who are watching you become.

Jack Platt: If you're going to enter a denied area, do your homework. What function is going on there? Let's say you find out they're serving champagne. I would come in through the back door carrying a case of champagne, saying, "This is a special order. Harry Patripsy wanted this special champagne for his table."

● EVERYDAY INFILTRATION

Let's see how to apply these rules to practical situations.
For instance, say you really need to use the "customers only"
restaurant bathroom. Here are the steps you might take:

1. Observe all the usual spy "invisibility" dictums: Conform
to dress and behavior norms for that restaurant, act
relaxed and purposeful.

2. Don't ask; they will just say no.

3. If a line of people is waiting for tables, get in line.
If they offer to seat you, say that you are waiting for
somebody. After a
decent interval,
go and conquer
that unguarded
beachhead.

4. If there's no line,
enter and scan the
tables looking for
a friend you're
"supposed to meet
there." Then go
through all the
expected motions:
check your watch,

your cell phone, etc. As long as you look like you've come in for the food and not the bathroom, there's almost no chance you will be challenged.

5. When you come out of the toilet, go through the motions of pretending you've had a sudden change of plans. Exit smoothly, not in a rush. You've just enjoyed the final movement in a symphony of lavatorial satisfaction, so why end it with a coda of aggravation?

6. If all else fails, go to Starbuck's like everybody else.

How about when you want to crash a party or exclusive club? Whether trying to glide past a velvet rope or a host you've never met, the first rule is to assume you will be successful. After all, hardly anybody is going to expend excessive effort just to foil a harmless crasher. As ex-CIA infiltratologist Jack Platt puts it, "You can't turn the place into a police state. You have to ask, 'What's the danger? What's the threat?' It's about security versus efficiency. Security is usually completely inefficient."

Again, the usual spy techniques of invisibility, utter confidence, and unflappability are probably all you'll need, but here are a few specific approaches:

PRETEND TO BE A MINION for someone legitimate. Find out the name of a person who has been invited or is important enough to breeze right in—don't choose a celebrity, because no one will believe you. Phone ahead to whoever

REFUSAL SHOES:

WHEN IMMIGRATION OFFICERS ARBITRARILY SEIZE UPON "INAPPROPRIATE FOOTWEAR" AS AN EXCUSE FOR DENYING ENTRY TO FOREIGNERS

PHRASE USED BY FORMER BRITISH IMMIGRATION OFFICER TONY SAINT IN HIS 2003 NOVEL OF THE SAME NAME

is responsible for the guest list, and explain (apologetically) that you are phoning from the invitee's office, and would be grateful if they could add another VIP to the list: the invitee's agent, brother... whatever seems appropriate. Leave an impressive-sounding but easy-to-spell false name.

PIGGY-BACKING. Merge into a group that is clearly destined for a warm welcome. Choose a crowd to which you might realistically belong: For example, if it's a rapper and his posse, and you've opted for the aging tycoon with a walrus mustache look, you might want to wait for another group. You might also check that you have the right address.

● SPY TECHNIQUES FOR COMMUNICATING

SPYING, LIKE A GOOD SOAP OPERA, is all about the learning and keeping of secrets. Spies learn secrets primarily by monitoring communications and recruiting agents to their cause. You really shouldn't be monitoring communications, and in everyday life the agent is replaced by a "gossip," but you have one advantage over a spy: You can often get close enough to your quarry to simply overhear what they are saying.

A spy rarely enjoys the luxury of old-fashioned eaves-dropping. Not only do her targets tend to be paranoid about voicing secrets in public, but also if she gets caught snooping, it might mean expulsion from the country, or worse.

Of course, some people have moral qualms about eaves-dropping. If you're one of them, then think of a conversation as a type of broadcast. If a broadcast is beamed over the public airwaves, then everybody is free to tune in. If it's performed in private, then you need to pay for that cable or satellite feed.

Likewise, if someone is thoughtless enough to pollute the communal air with his prattling, then he has no right to demand that bystanders make any effort to tune out. But if that person has gone to the trouble of scrambling the signal (i.e., conducting the conversation under what one would reasonably expect to be private circumstances), then if you hijack that transmission you are a violator—and there is no equivalent of "paying the cable guy 50 bucks."

So how do you avoid that embarrassment? The way a spy listens in on nearby conversations is to sit as close as possible and hold a decoy conversation with another person, throwing the target off the scent. Now, it's almost impossible, you might interject here, to hold a conversation while trying to focus on another. Yes, we reply, and so that is why the spy has a concealed device recording the adjacent conversation. That way she doesn't miss a thing, nor is she suspected of snooping.

● GUARDING YOUR CONVERSATION

Inside the Soviet Bloc during the Cold War, the comedy stereotype of finding a blatant microphone in every hotel room and at the Johnny Foreigner table in the few restaurants open to Westerners wasn't too far from the truth. Spies learned either to clam up entirely or to speak in code.

▮▮▮▮ CODES VS. CIPHERS ▮▮▮▮

With a code, entire words or even sentences are substituted for what is meant. For example, somebody extremely boring asks you and your partner to dinner. If you've pre-arranged a *code,* you might turn to your partner and say, "Gee, honey, don't we have that, er, *thing?*" And your partner might respond, "That *what?* Oh, right, that *thing.* That darn *thing* that precludes us from having such an interesting dinner."

In fact, you have used the word "thing" as a code—a substitute for "overwhelming need to get as far from this guy as possible," and "interesting" to mean "excruciatingly dull."

A less handy device is a *cipher,* which works by replacing individual letters. Ordinarily you would need to sit down with a cipher key (or a computer) to crack a ciphered message. So in the above scenario, for example, you might hand a piece of paper to your partner upon which is written "OP XBZ!" You have transposed each letter to the letter in the alphabet that follows. Thus your message, understandable to your partner but not to a third party, actually reads, "No way!" And once again you have both prevented somebody from being offended and evaded a potentially unpleasant evening—the spy way.

HISTORICAL CODES AND CIPHERS

Ancient Roman gangsta Julius Caesar would use a simple displacement cipher to encode correspondence with government officials and friends. He replaced each letter with the letter that follows alphabetically by three places. Thus, when he famously uttered, "Et tu Brute," which of course are three nonsense words, what he really meant was, "Bq Qr Yorqb"—the sound of a man searching for meaning in a world that's just jabbed him in the gut.

A French agent in Indochina during its World War II occupation by the Japanese decided to shave his dog and write his report in indelible ink on the surface of the hairless dog. The agent waited for the dog's fur to grow back, and then he and the pooch fled the country. Unfortunately, the dog-hide report wasn't filed until a year after the fact, and by then the information was deemed obsolete.

You might consider toning down or encoding the personal information you're leaking to the world. At times, we all have reasons for shielding our discourse that go beyond a mere craving for privacy. Such as:

- ❏ Protecting a creative idea or business secret
- ❏ Disguising your nationality in a hostile environment
- ❏ Discussing a purchase with an associate without betraying to the seller your level of interest or maximum offer
- ❏ Preventing everybody in the joint from over-hearing your phone number, email address, or credit card details when you need to reveal it to somebody

● CONCEALMENT

HAVE YOU EVER TAKEN a bottle of good wine to a house party and then not been able to find it amidst all the other "fine wines" under $5 on display at the communal table? Your host

IN THE 1970s the U.S. NAVY and the NSA launched OPERATION IVY BELLS, which planted a bug on a Soviet underwater communications cable between the major NAVAL BASES of Vladivostok and Petropavlovsk. The Navy sent in a team of COMBAT DIVERS to tap the undersea cable by installing a "wraparound" device that recorded all communications transmitted through the line. This mission continued successfully until the SOVIETS discovered it in 1981. How did they find out? In 1985, U.S. authorities arrested RONALD W. PELTON, a former NSA EMPLOYEE who had SOLD OUT the CABLE-TAPPING operation to the Soviets for $35,000, chump change for the damage done.

has learned the time-honored art of hiding. But being good at hiding isn't only for caching the decent vino. It can also prevent burglars from purloining your valuables at home.

A popular and effective way to hide small valuables is placing them inside a hollowed-out food package, beauty product, or book, which you can fashion yourself, if you've got the knack, or can purchase pre-made. Burglars generally haven't the time or inclination to scrutinize the mundane—after all, they didn't

smash a window and climb into a strange house to steal a can of shaving cream. Two keys to making this system work are:

❑ Use only common, name-brand products. If it looks fake or generic it might attract attention.

❑ Don't forget what you've done and end up tossing away your engagement ring in the next spring cleaning.

If you're feeling particularly vulnerable, you might want to consider hollowing out a piece of heavy furniture and stashing your valuables inside.

Jack Platt explains where a trained spy would look for concealed valuables: "I'd look for something out of the ordinary. For example, if you see a non-smoker has a big, heavy stone ashtray, you should examine that ashtray. Or if you see a row of history books, such as the Winston Churchill series, and then in the middle of them is *The Sex Life of a Midget,* I'd want to pull that book down and see if it's been hollowed out."

● DEAD DROPS

ONCE AN AGENT has been put into play by a field operative, the pair will rarely meet again face to face. Instead, they correspond by leaving messages and materials at predetermined sites called "dead drops." The operative might leave instructions for future meetings, personal messages, questions or requests, specialized equipment such as a micro-camera, and money or some other form of compensation. The agent might leave correspondence and secret materials.

The operative and agent each indicate to the other that something is waiting in the "dead letter box" of the next dead-drop site by leaving a marking of some sort at a predetermined signal site. These signals are commonly as simple as a chalk or lipstick mark or piece of colored string on a telephone pole or mailbox. Different signals might indicate, for example, that a planned dead drop has been cancelled because it is too dangerous.

The local spy station will do advance reconnaissance of the area and choose a number of spots that are appropriate for dead drops and signals. Each dead drop and signalling site is given a specific code name so that both agent and handler will clearly know where the next one is meant to take place.

You may not need to leave secret aircraft blueprints for your pals, but how about a set of keys to your house or car? The principles of the dead drop apply to such everyday situations.

TIPS FOR CHOOSING A DEAD DROP LOCATION

1. It must be easy to describe and find.

2. It must be secure, well concealed from casual onlookers, and not overlooked by any windows. Avoid places where children play, gardeners work, tramps congregate, or enemy spies walk their nosy dogs.

3. It must allow for the safe deposit and removal of material. Operatives must be able to check whether they are being watched.

4. It must be located out of the weather and accessible at any time of day or night.

5. The location must be in line with the participants' public image and legends. A burger joint, for example, would be a poor dead-drop site for a supposed vegetarian.

HOW TO PREPARE MATERIALS FOR A DEAD DROP

1. **When digging a hole** or hollowing out a tree, just
   remember that old lyric, "Night time is the right time."

2. **Either figure out a way to describe** the dead drop
   exactly, or draw a map. Work out a signal system for
   yourself and your agent indicating when the material
   has been deposited and when it has been removed.
   A popular signal for non-spies might be a chalk or
   lipstick mark on a park bench—or a telephone call.
   Hmm, yes, probably a telephone call.

■ ■ ■ ■ ■ MATA HARI'S HEAD ■ ■ ■ ■ ■

Nowadays when you imagine a spy there's a 50-50 chance you'll picture a woman. But in the past, spying, like most other action pursuits, was perceived as the province of men. So when a woman spy came along, she had the advantage of being unexpected.

Dutch-born Mata Hari had a sexy image that belied her bleak career spying for the French against the Germans—and then possibly vice versa—during World War I. She was executed by a French firing squad in 1917. Mata Hari's head was then removed, mummified, and eventually put on display at the Museum of Anatomy, in Paris. In July 2000, officials discovered that someone had stolen Mata's head. Why was the head taken? It is not known whether the head has been grafted onto another body, revivified, and sent back out into the cold world of spying once again—though it is doubtful.

3. **Devise a safe route** to and from the dead drop, as well as a cover story for being there in case you are caught.

4. **Place the item in a jar,** or wrap it in plastic or some other weatherproof container. You might even consider affixing the item to metal using a magnet or a magnetized flat box that can hold keys. For the

non-cynical, fake garden rocks are available with decoy inspirational messages, like "Create!." Just be sure to place it amidst other rocks in a natural setting.

5. Deposit the item at the dead drop.

6. Leave a signal that the item is ready to be collected. This signal should not be within the vicinity of the dead drop. Also, minimize the amount of time that the material is sitting at the dead drop.

● ROBERT HANSSEN: MASTER OF THE DEAD DROP

IN 2001, the FBI finally nabbed one of the most damaging turncoats in American history. Robert Hanssen spent the last fifteen of his twenty-five years as a highly placed counter-intelligence officer for the FBI supplying a frightening amount of sensitive material to Soviet, and later, Russian intelligence.

If there's one statistic that certifies the quality and quantity of American secrets that Hanssen betrayed, it's the alleged $1.4 million in cash and diamonds that he received from the notoriously tight-fisted Russkies. (If you recall the case of *The Falcon and the Snowman,* those guys were paid in beer money.)

Hanssen left more than 20 dead drops for his Russian handlers in various Virginia parks. He would bundle the material securely in weatherproof plastic, then affix it to the underside of bridges. The information he allegedly divulged was mind-boggling. It included:

❑ Details of a secret U.S. surveillance tunnel under
the Russian Embassy that had cost several hundred
million dollars to build.

❑ Names of Russians working in Moscow for the CIA.

❑ The "continuity of government" plan, in which top
American leaders would convene in a secret bunker
during a nuclear first strike.

Hanssen's story is rife with bizarre details:

❑ Ten years before he was finally arrested, his brother-
in-law, who was also an FBI agent, reported him as a
possible traitor, but the FBI didn't pursue the case.

❑ Hanssen's wife, Bonnie, reportedly once caught him
in the act of preparing documents and compelled
him to see a priest. The priest advised Hanssen to
donate his blood money to charity, and so Hanssen
turned his Russian booty over to Mother Teresa.

❑ Hanssen, a deeply religious father of six, had a
relationship with a stripper, giving her presents
including a Mercedes and an AmEx account, and
even took her on an FBI assignment to Hong Kong.

❑ Hanssen, a master of subterfuge, nonetheless
posted his sexual fantasies on websites under his
own name and with his actual email address.

Finally, a daring spy obtained Hanssen's KGB file and
handed it over to the FBI. Undercover agents moved into the
house opposite Hanssen's and began surveillance, placing a

CARLOS THE JACKAL embarked on a twenty-year killing spree that started with the Palestinian terrorist attack at the 1972 Munich Olympics. He would go on to commit a series of car BOMBINGS in France that killed dozens and injured hundreds. In 1975, he seized seventy HOSTAGES at a meeting in VIENNA of oil ministers from OPEC. For most of the 1970s and early 1980s, Venezuelan-born Ilich Ramirez Sanchez was wanted for TERRORIST crimes in at least five European countries. To evade intelligence agencies around the world, he relied on forged passports, replacing the owner's photo with his own and FORGING the bearer's signature. He was finally captured in Sudan in 1994, and sentenced to three life terms in prison.

transmitter in his car. Hanssen apparently knew the FBI was on to him, but he still didn't quit. At Foxstone Park, a quiet park near his home in Vienna, Virginia—known to his Russian handlers as Dead Drop Ellis—Hanssen deposited his last package under a footbridge, and then he was arrested.

Hanssen pleaded guilty to avoid the death penalty, so no charges were ever publicly filed and no trial was ever held. He was sentenced to life imprisonment.

SMELLING A RAT

It doesn't take a cat-stroking übervillain to cast a pall over an otherwise pleasant day. Much more likely is some greasy reprobate rooting through your trash cans for credit card or Social Security numbers. Spies are a wary lot, and you can learn a few practical tips from the way that they perceive and then contend with evil. You may not be licensed to kill, but you can employ other, less terminal spy techniques to thwart everyone from the shoulder surfer at the ATM to the early-rising neighbor who's filching your morning newspaper to the bogus meter reader with a keen ability to hastily assess the value of your home-entertainment system. That's not to mention the photo jock who has mounted a hidden camera in the rest room.

This chapter will teach you how to protect yourself from the societal dregs who would steal your money, your sense of security, even your identity. It will help you cope with the abuse of privacy-invading technologies. You don't have to mistrust everybody you encounter, but you can use your spy eye to look out for trouble.

BONA FIDES: PROOF OF A PERSON'S CLAIMED IDENTITY

● FALSE IDENTITIES

ONE WAY TO MAKE ANY TRANSACTION, be it social or business, more secure is to positively identify the parties with whom you're dealing. That way, if something should go awry, you have recourse to official avenues of complaint, including civil and criminal courts. But you'll end up with only frustration if you get swindled and the perpetrator of the scam was not who you thought he was.

The CIA's former Vietnam–based interrogator John Sullivan tells how he separates the flim from the flam: "Let's say someone presents himself as an insurance salesman. First, I'd ask for ID. If he doesn't have any, I'd ask for a telephone number I can call to check on him. Anyone who's trying to misrepresent himself is not going to supply bona fides I can check with a phone call.

"In a social situation, if a person comes up to me and says, for example, 'I was in Vietnam,' then I have no doubt I could ferret this out. If someone were presenting himself as a Harvard graduate, and talked like someone who hadn't graduated from high school, I'd ask, 'What year did you graduate? Were you in the Hasty Pudding Club? Did you know so and so (with a made-up name)?' If he says yes to the made-up name, I've got him. Otherwise he's given me enough to check on later if necessary.

"If someone just showed up at my door, I would try to ask questions the answers to which I already know. No matter who you're trying to verify, you should always try to find common touchstones—questions that you can answer and that he should certainly know."

HIGH FASHION CAN ALSO BE USEFUL. Female spies have long used their clothing, including BUTTONS and BONNETS, to transport messages across enemy lines. Rose O'Neal Greenhow, famous as "REBEL ROSE" during the Civil War, sent young BETTY DUVALL on a mission with a SECRET LETTER carried in her CHIGNON. In a later war, JOSEPHINE BAKER smuggled photographs and sheet music with hidden messages in her dresses.

● IDENTITY THEFT

IDENTITY THEFT IS THE HOT CRIME of the new millennium, and it's easy to see why. For better or worse, globalization and the internet have helped drive many markets toward their ultimate efficiencies—and as economist Adam Smith explained over two hundred years ago, this is where markets like to go.

A byproduct of this is that we spend a good part of our lives doing business and socializing with people we may never meet—and who might know us by our phone numbers or email addresses, but wouldn't be able to positively identify us in a line-up with our email addresses tattooed on our foreheads.

And so unfurls the crime of our times—stealing the identity of another for purposes of obtaining goods or committing crimes under that pseudonym. Identity theft has been growing steadily. It affects an estimated 500,000 Americans per year, and it's incredibly easy to perpetrate—and yet even people

> ## "The 'wilderness of mirrors' is an ever fluid landscape where fact and illusion merge."
>
> — JAMES JESUS ANGLETON,
> former Chief of the CIA Counterintelligence Staff

who are extremely security conscious about their material possessions and physical safety leave themselves wide open to it. Obviously, no spy would be taken so easily, and neither should you—so take a few tips from the people who believe that the best identity is no identity at all.

HOW DO THEY DO IT?

A professional identity thief begins with a few key bits of information, such as name, address, place of birth, mother's maiden name, or Social Security number. From this she obtains a "breeder document"—an easy-to-obtain record, such as a birth certificate, that can be used to acquire others. From there it's relatively straightforward to amass a wallet full of valid ID cards under a false name. If the thief is truly determined, she can obtain credit cards, loans, a driver's license, and a passport under your name. She can even get a job using your name and Social Security number, and leave *you* liable for taxes due on *her* earnings. *Ouch.*

Here's how they do it:

1. DUMPSTER DIVING.

Identity theft often begins at the corporate dumpster and the home garbage can. Corporate divers are looking for letterheads, job descriptions, memos, internal phone directories —anything that gives them rosters and insights into the workings of a company. Players of the home version of the game are looking for pay slips, bank statements, credit card receipts—anything that gives them account numbers, Social Security numbers—the building blocks of an identity profile.

2. DIGITAL DATA.

Even if you don't fall prey to one of their schemes, hackers can ferret out personal information stored internally by websites or on company networks. Also, dishonest technicians can still retrieve information from discarded disks or computer hard drives even if the files were deleted.

The moral is: Don't sell or give away your used computer to anybody who is obviously crooked.

3. INSIDE JOBS. Everybody who works for or has access to any company that stores personal data has the world at her fingertips. You can't do much about this, other than to limit your exposure by keeping things simple: By not applying for every charge card that's offered, not giving away information on websites or when entering "contests," and by moving to Antarctica to live amongst the penguins.

BURN BAG: A TRASH BAG OF CONFIDENTIAL PAPERS THAT HAVE BEEN EARMARKED FOR DESTRUCTION BY PULPING OR BURNING

● WHAT CAN YOU DO?

1. **SHRED.** Even unsolicited junk mail is a danger— do you really want some bandit filling out every credit card application that you've tossed? Shred all credit-card and ATM receipts, everything with bank account or Social Security numbers on it. Cut up old credit cards, including right across your raised name.

2. **KEEP ADDRESS CURRENT.** Make sure that everyone you can think of who might send you mail is up-to-date on your current address. Better to have more junk mail to shred than to have misdirected mail— packed with your vital stats—floating about for the creepy new tenant to see.

3. CLAM UP. It seems so obvious, but enough people are willing to divulge their key info to strangers that "preying upon the trusting" is now a growth industry in America. If they don't have a need to know, don't reveal things about yourself that can be used to defraud you.

4. BEWARE OF UNSOLICITED emails and websites. No legitimate website will send you an email and either ask you to reply directly with personal details or to click on a link in the email and enter private information. Just as you should

only give out information over the phone to strangers when you have made the call, *you* should enter details on websites only when *you* have steered yourself to the site.

5. PASSWORDS. Most people are really stupid about their passwords—someone who barely knows you could try to log onto different sites with your email address and your pet's name, your street address, or your favorite sports team—if that's what you chose for your password.

■ ■ ■ ■ ■ ■ THE CASE OF ■ ■ ■ ■ ■ ■
THE UNBURNED COOKIE WRAPPERS

In 1970 in Saigon, U.S. Naval Intelligence was alerted that top-secret papers from a burn bag were not being destroyed, but were instead being sold by a Vietnamese national employed by the Navy to a so-called "Cookie Lady." Suspecting this was some sort of code name, an alarmed investigating officer tracked the case to a street corner, where the suspect was in fact peddling cookies —and wrapping them in confidential Navy documents.

It turned out that neither the Cookie Lady nor her supplier could read English, and simply found the documents to be functional for wrapping. We don't know if they were fortune cookies, but if they were, we have a pretty good idea what the one for the person responsible for burn-bag security must've said.

ANTI-THEFT MEASURES

ATMS AND SHOULDER SURFERS

The ATM is truly one of the great conveniences of the modern world. And thanks to daily withdrawal limits and sporadic on-site security, it's a relatively low-risk one at that—at least when fending off the common criminal. But you also need to counter the new breed of tech-savvy no-goodniks who specialize in ATM crime.

ATM crime is usually a two-step process: acquiring your ATM card and learning your PIN. Both of these are accomplished without your ever knowing it.

STEALING YOUR CARD

The most popular method is to trap your card in the ATM slot. The thief then waits until you have departed to retrieve the card. New gizmos for this are constantly being invented, so you have to assume you are always going to be one step behind the criminal tech curve.

They might install a phony ATM in a public space for a few hours, especially at night. Guess what — no money, no card, nobody to complain to.

Some criminals affix a card-reading device or "skimmer" over the slot of an authentic ATM. You use the ATM as normal and even get your card back and your money, but the skimmer records your account number and PIN. They can then clone your card, and you might not realize what has happened — until you get your next bank statement.

STEALING YOUR PIN

The most common method is "shoulder surfing," or reading a password or PIN over your shoulder.

Being "helpful." If your card gets stuck, the guy offering to assist you might just be a Good Samaritan, but if he advises you to re-enter your PIN, it's a good bet he's not.

Criminals have been known to watch from a vehicle or an alcove nearby with high-powered binoculars or a video camera. In a few cases, criminals have even installed a tiny camera just above the ATM's keypad.

HOW TO COMBAT THEFT

If your card gets stuck in a machine:

- ❑ Don't repeatedly re-enter your PIN. You won't get your cash tonight, but at least you won't give the guy too close behind you in line another chance to learn your PIN.
- ❑ Cancel the card immediately, ideally by cell phone while you are still standing by the ATM. Don't let anybody else use the ATM until you have canceled your card.
- ❑ Don't use the machine if you see any abnormal add-ons, particularly above the card slot.
- ❑ Beware of anyone "repairing" the machine at off hours—no bank is going to pay overtime for this.

BLACK OPERATIONS:
COVERT OPERATIONS THAT ARE NOT ATTRIBUTABLE TO THE PARTY PERFORMING THEM

CHARLES FRASER-SMITH, a brilliant inventor of spy devices for MI-6, was the inspiration for Ian Fleming's **Q** in the JAMES BOND novels. Smith's creations—weapons and tools disguised as ordinary objects—were known as "**Q**" DEVICES, named after the "Q" ships of WWI, which were WARSHIPS disguised as ordinary vessels. Among the objects he crafted was a PEN containing a SECRET COMPARTMENT for a tiny map and a magnetized clip that was balanced on a pin to provide an emergency compass. He devised PAPER IMPREGNATED with a MAGNESIUM compound that would BURN INSTANTLY, leaving almost no ash. Another gadget was a CIGARETTE HOLDER TELESCOPE, complete with nicotine stains.

❑ Always enter your PIN discreetly. Be like a spy and check out the various angles from which someone might be watching. Cover the keypad with your other hand—it's low-tech, to be sure, but so is PIN stealing.

● LOW-LEVEL THEFT

What? Use spy techniques to combat trivial, everyday annoyances? Let's put it this way. There's nothing more satisfying than catching a weasel who thinks he's getting away with some petty crime. Well, there probably are a few things more satisfying, like bringing a genocidal maniac to justice, or kicking cancer, or winning a Nobel prize . . . Nope, we take it back—this is as good as it gets.

HOW TO LAY A TRAP FOR WHOEVER IS STEALING YOUR FOOD FROM THE FRIDGE IN THE BREAK ROOM

The trick to this is sacrifice. You can catch the culprit first time out, but you have to forego refrigerated food that day. Simply choose a treat that you know will be popular with the food thief, package it attractively, and add some well-camouflaged extra seasoning. *(Definitely not rat poison or anything radioactive – we cannot stress this enough. Or anything "just lying around" if you happen to work at the Centers for Disease Control.)* For example, a dash of hot cayenne pepper is perfect for an instant identification, but it needs to be concealed in something red—ketchup, for example. A spicy mouthful later, the guilty party will be panting for forgiveness.

HOW TO STOP A LIGHT-FINGERED NEIGHBOR

Conflict with neighbors is especially tricky, but you can halt poaching behavior without having to resort to direct confrontation. Whether your neighbors are lifting the coupon section out of your newspaper or "dead-heading" your prize roses, a spy's greatest weapon is stealth. Strike hard, then disappear without a trace. A spy would never want to attack a savvy target who knows her identity and where she lives. Why make a dangerous and motivated enemy who possesses a vantage point from which to track your daily movements? So in this case, you're going for a ceasing of offensive activity rather than capturing and punishing the offender.

Your neighbor is probably perpetrating these acts under cover of darkness or when nobody is about. So you need to negate both of these opportunities. We recommend illumination . . . and irony.

BLACK BAG JOB: UNAUTHORIZED ENTRY INTO A HOME OR OFFICE TO STEAL OR COPY MATERIALS

ILLUMINATION. A small floodlight with a motion sensor might not deter a professional thief, but it will startle an opportunist into leaving well enough alone. Place one aimed right between your houses—and see the human raccoon run.

IRONY. A spy rarely gets a chance to exercise irony, except for 007's occasional dry commentaries. But in this case it might be your most effective tactic. By placing little signs near the oft-pilfered items, such as PLEASE STEAL THIS ONE, DEAR NEIGHBOR (yes, "irony" can also be a fancy word for "sarcasm"), your neighbor will be shamed into retreat.

USING SPY TECHNIQUES TO MAINTAIN YOUR PRIVACY

The Cold War was the Golden Age of Snooping. In those days of primitive technology, snooping meant hiding as best you could a microphone on the person or in the vicinity of a target from the other side, especially in the

■ ■ ■ ■ ■ THE ROSENBERGS: ■ ■ ■ ■ ■
LOVE, DEATH, AND NUCLEAR SECRETS

Some neighbors don't settle for merely stealing the morning paper. New Yorkers Julius and Ethel Rosenberg were the only American civilians to be executed for espionage during the Cold War. Convicted of conspiring to pass U.S. nuclear secrets to the KGB, the couple was at the center of a spy network that included Ethel's brother David Greenglass, a Los Alamos technician working on the atomic bomb.

When Julius refused to talk after being caught, the FBI arrested Ethel too, in hopes of breaking her husband. Their trial rested heavily on testimony supplied by Greenglass, who was spared execution in exchange for his testimony. The arrangement led many to think the charges were trumped up in an era of anti-Communist hysteria. Nevertheless, top-secret KGB cables known as the Venona Papers were finally released in 1995, providing conclusive evidence against Julius Rosenberg. Nikita Khrushchev, in his memoirs, said, "The Rosenbergs provided very significant help in accelerating the production of our atomic bomb."

limited number of hotel rooms and restaurants made available to Westerners behind the Iron Curtain. Although audio snooping is still employed, the miniaturization of digital video means that today's bug is detected far less easily. And video surveillance is one spy technique that has been widely adopted in our everyday life.

In Great Britain, video surveillance via what are known as CCTV cameras are presently monitoring public areas in over 300 cities and towns. Sharp reductions in crime have been reported. In Northhampton, crime decreased by 57 percent, and in Glasgow, Scotland, it decreased by 68 percent Although these cameras, usually mounted on 20-foot poles, do help solve crimes, the fact that they are so ubiquitous in British life has to disquiet anybody concerned with privacy. The ghost of George Orwell is smiling.

In many developed countries, omnipresent CCTV cameras are now a fact of life. And while they're designed to catch evildoers in the act, benign uses for CCTV, such as monitoring traffic jams or allowing office workers to check the level of the break-room coffee pot, ensure that we're never far from an involuntary photo op.

The trade-off between security and privacy can be endlessly debated, but the reality is that we'd all better get used to it. And just as James Bond foiled the sexy snooper, Pussy Galore, in the airplane bathroom in *Goldfinger* by covering up the peepholes, we too can protect ourselves from being abused via video by using—that's right—spy techniques.

EXAMPLES OF VIDEO ABUSE

1. AN EMPLOYER uses intrusive cameras that are ostensibly protecting against theft and monitoring productivity to violate an employee's basic rights of personal privacy.

2. CELL PHONES WITH CAMERAS are being used to photograph in restricted areas like factories, businesses, and museums—the pictures are then used for research or to steal intellectual property.

3. DIGITAL CAMERAS with modern large storage capacities have been installed and left to be collected much later. The shrinking of cameras plus the elimination of the need for telltale cables or frequent maintenance has made it even easier for the voyeur to ply his trade undetected.

4. VOYEURS PLANT secret, illegal cameras in locker rooms, public showers, clothing-store fitting rooms, and bathrooms. This last perpetration is widely known as a "Johnny B. Bad," in homage to a certain rock & roll legend who in 1990 paid a large settlement after being accused in a class-action suit of filming two hundred women in the toilet at his home and at his restaurant.

5. ANOTHER MORE VOYEURISTIC example is using a cell camera to "up-shoot" photos under the skirts of unsus-

pecting women. In response to widespread incidents, especially in Japan, manufacturers have added the traditional (and technically unnecessary) sound of a camera shutter to these units to help expose perpetrators.

HOW CAMERAS ARE HIDDEN

DISTANCE. The camera can be mounted high up or far away, with a telescopic lens.

BELOW EYE LEVEL, tilted upward.

BEHIND TWO-WAY MIRRORS, such as in stores, nightclubs, and casinos.

WITHIN MOUNTED FIXTURES, such as in lights, smoked-glass domes, fans, smoke detectors, and sprinklers.

THROUGH HOLES drilled in walls or ceilings.

THROUGH VENTILATION grills.

WITHIN MOTION SENSORS OR INFRARED SENSORS, such as in automatic sink taps, toilets, hand dryers, and remote-control receptors in TVs and other electronics.

HOW TO DETECT HIDDEN CAMERAS

Here are some telltale clues that can alert you to the presence of surveillance activity:

- ❏ A public area is overly lit for no apparent reason.
- ❏ Fixtures exist that seem to serve no purpose, such as lamps that are turned off at night or fans that aren't operational on a hot day.
- ❏ A two-way mirror is concealing a camera. You can confirm it by getting up close and blocking out the light with your hands—you should be able to see through the mirror.
- ❏ Dumb-looking smoked-glass globes are hanging from the ceiling.
- ❏ Some really lame voyeurs have failed to cover the little red recording light.

Granted, your chances of coming under surveillance may seem small now. But with the rising concerns about terrorism comes the increasing use of monitoring equipment that tracks not only car bombers but ordinary citizens as well. That's not to mention criminals with some technical know-how. You can combat these intrusions in your life. Spies operate at all times as though eyes are upon them. You can too, and keep things you want to be private to yourself.

IN 1984, GEORGE ORWELL'S masterpiece, the GOVERNMENT ENLISTS everyone, even children, as INFORMERS. A real-life variation of this occurred shortly after World War II, when a group of RUSSIAN schoolchildren gave the U.S. AMBASSADOR, Averell Harriman, a "token of friendship": a carved wooden REPLICA of the Great Seal of the United States. The ambassador regarded it as a SYMBOL of the friendship between the two countries. There was only one problem. Six years later, in 1952, TECHNICIANS DISCOVERED a small bugging device inside.

CHAPTER

8

TAKING YOUR SPY BRAIN
ON THE ROAD

The classic spy is a field operative, traveling in a hostile area with unknown factors on all sides, mistrusting even innocent-looking bystanders, unable to eat a meal without the threat of poisoning in the back of his mind, forced to change travel plans at a moment's notice, subject at any time to a thorough frisking and interrogation. Do you see where we're going with this? That's right—it's just like being on a typical business trip.

Traveling is one area where a spy's life truly parallels an average Joe's. All of us at one time or another will find ourselves in a strange place, one where we don't know anybody, don't know our way around, and aren't sure which areas are safe and which are dangerous. And the post-9/11 twist is that traveling to this risky place is now even scarier than actually being there.

That is where spy techniques come in. Because these are exactly the sorts of dangers that beset spies, their well-proven practices, techniques, and rules of thumb can make every trip a smooth ride.

IN THE DANGER ZONE

IT WASN'T SO LONG AGO that danger zones were well-defined. To detect whether you were in one, you could simply ask:

- ❑ Is there a war going on here?
- ❑ Are armed thugs running rampant in the streets?
- ❑ How about large mammals with razor-sharp incisors?
- ❑ Testing any nuclear devices here today?
- ❑ Was this sudden overcast caused by a cloud or a plummeting asteroid?

Nowadays, in our terror-charged climate, danger can truly lurk everywhere—especially on all means of public transportation. So, if you absorbed the message earlier in this book about increasing your awareness in everyday life, then you'd be a complete fool not to multiply that awareness many times over when you are in transit to or after you have arrived at a strange place. We don't all get the PDB (President's Daily Brief), so pay attention to details and keep that spy brain engaged.

Different parts of the world have raised awarenesses for different threats; the key for the future is for *all* of us to be aware of *all* manner of threats. For example, the English have for decades been hyper-vigilant of unattended packages and vehicles, because this is how the IRA waged its bombing campaign. To this day, tourists are perplexed not to find any garbage bins in stations of the London Underground; they've been permanently removed for security purposes. Likewise, nobody is more aware of the profile of a potential suicide bomber than an Israeli.

Awareness of others should extend to being aware of how others perceive you. You may know that you are harmless, but it's now become your responsibility to convey this message to the general public. Common courtesy, in addition to the desire to avoid a full body-cavity search, behooves you to observe a modicum of thoughtfulness.

Jeannette Hyde, travel editor of the UK's *Observer* newspaper, was at Oslo airport in April 2004 when a man parked a suitcase in a check-in line and then departed. Presumably he was holding his place while going back curbside to say his good-byes or retrieve another bag. A few years earlier, this action would have likely been ignored. But within seconds, Hyde writes, panic set in. The man was almost lynched by jittery passengers upon his return. And this was in *Oslo*.

● ON FOREIGN GROUND

ONCE YOU HAVE ARRIVED at your destination, using spy rules can prevent you from being targeted as another slack-jawed tourist with mouth agape at the sights. That happens to be the type of victim that attracts local thieves looking for easy prey. Interviews with criminals consistently show that more than gender, age, size, or socioeconomic group, crooks target those who seem unaware of their surroundings. Within five to fifteen seconds, a mugger will determine whether he can surprise you.

Here's how to avoid being a neon sign that flashes: "Take my wallet! Take my purse!"

1. Take your cues on dressing from the locals. For extended journeys, consider packing ultra-light and buying cheap, indigenous clothing at your destination. Leave behind any clothes that will brand you as an American—cowboy hats and boots, American flag-emblazoned t-shirts, big white athletic shoes, and neon-colored jogging suits.

2. Don't wear ostentatious jewelry, not even costume jewelry, because, believe it or not, you might encounter a mugger who can't tell a karat from a carrot.

3. Keep your voice down. Don't stand out—blend in. Americans are notorious for this—they're known world-wide for braying stridently and dressing loudly, untidily and immodestly. They even walk and sit differently. Try to picture yourself through the ears and eyes of people around you.

4. Carry your shopping and personal items discreetly, in a container similar to that of the locals. For example, throughout Eastern Europe, shopping and even work items are generally carried in large plastic shopping bags rather than backpacks, briefcases, or satchels. In particular, don't carry bags with showy brands that mark you as a foreigner.

5. Many thieves are simpletons, dazzled by the new and shiny. So place high-value items, such as computers or cameras, in dirty and scuffed old bags.

put away that map

keep voice down

hide your wallet

wear indigenous clothing

no ostentatious jewelry

computers and cameras in here

use plastic shopping bag not backpack

6. Hide your wallet, cash, and passport in a money belt or thin pouch under your shirt. Keep only a small amount of money readily available in your pockets or bag.

7. Put away that map! Try to plot out your way before you leave the hotel room. If you must have a peek, stop in populated squares or avenues.

HOW TO NAVIGATE MEAN STREETS

On your home turf, you know which streets to avoid and which to use. Whether you're aware of it or not, you walk with a certain confidence fueled by familiarity. You're in your comfort zone.

But when you're on the road, it's a different story. You can't tell from a map which streets are perfumed with lavender and which ones reek of cabbage. Is that green patch a place for an evening stroll— or Needle Park? And if you're inside a strange place, even a mall with familiar brand names, a disco, or a movie theater, do you know how to get out fast in case of emergency? Here are some tips on steering out of harm's way on the mean streets.

KEEP A LOW PROFILE. Act like you know where you are and where you're going, even if you've been wandering in circles for an hour.

STICK TO "STREETS WITH EYES" — multipurpose roads containing a variety of businesses. Don't be tempted into shortcuts that take you away from busier streets.

WALK IN THE MIDDLE OF THE SIDEWALK. Face traffic so that, for example, someone can't race up from behind on a moped or bicycle and surprise you.

NEVER CUT THE CORNER — it's the most vulnerable portion of any walk, and a perfect spot for a mugger to jump you.

RECONNOITER LARGE LOCATIONS where things can get scary in a jiffy: Locate the exits, the security, and potential problem areas.

NEVER ASSUME bystanders will come to your aid or even phone for help. You may be the latest installment in a familiar spectator sport.

You can have your spy brain fully engaged, you can be a virtual ghost, and yet still local goons can sniff you out.

SLEEPER:

AGENT LIVING AS AN ORDINARY CITIZEN IN A FOREIGN COUNTRY; ACTS ONLY WHEN ACTIVATED FOR AN OPERATION

If you are mugged, the most important thing to remember is that they do this for a living, so they're going to be better at it than you are. Don't try to fight your way out. Try to comply as much as possible on your terms. Here's how to manage the situation and get away without getting hurt.

1. Prepare a "giveaway wallet." Think of this as the civilian equivalent of a spy's decoy. It should be a cheap wallet containing not your actual credit cards or ID, but such items as store courtesy cards and expired, meaningless ID cards (e.g., "Spice Girls Fan Club") that might look legitimate on a quick glance by a jumpy, nervous assailant. Stock it with enough cash to satisfy a mugger that his time hasn't been wasted.

2. Carry the giveaway wallet in the pocket side of your weaker hand, leaving the good one free for defending yourself.

3. Carry enough cash hidden elsewhere on your person to pay for a taxi back to where you are staying.

4. Don't "throw down" the wallet—this might only enrage your attacker. Hand it over gingerly with your weaker hand.

5. As you hand it over, slowly step back and pivot away from the mugger, offering him the narrowest and least vulnerable target.

6. Slowly increase your distance from the mugger. Don't run immediately, because you'll probably spook the guy. Plus, if you turn your back he could assault you from behind. Slowly back off, then run or at least hasten away.

7. Find the nearest safe haven—some place where people are congregating and that provides a means of communication.

8. If you are inclined to carry a purse (no judgments here), hold it slightly forward, hands firmly on the straps, with the zipped zipper pull in front of your body. Credit cards, ID, and ready cash should be in another, less accessible pocket. Chic open back packs should be left at home.

9. Women should wear shoes that allow a quick getaway; leave the Manolos at home. Adjust your walking gait so that it is somewhat aggressive and act crazy if you have to.

EXFILTRATION: A CLANDESTINE RESCUE OPERATION TO BRING A DEFECTOR, REFUGEE, OR AN OPERATIVE AND FAMILY OUT OF A FOREIGN COUNTRY

WHAT IF SOMEBODY TRIES TO GET YOU TO GO SOMEWHERE ELSE WITH THEM?

It's one thing to be relieved of some money, a cell phone, or personal items. It's quite another to be assaulted, injured, or killed. Shakespeare said, "Who steals my purse steals trash"— this might be a bit of bravado, but it is basically sound. Surrender your stuff, but not your body. Once you've lost control of the situation, it will only get worse. Never let anybody take you anywhere. Your best hope is that they are afraid to assault you in public. Fight tooth and nail to remain in public.

LOCAL TRANSIT: SUBWAYS, TRAINS, AND BUSES

We are all country mice when visiting strange cities. Yet the rules that keep us safe at home apply to places where people talk funny and we don't know the way to the grocery store. Tap that spy noggin of yours and use common sense:

1. DON'T READ on the train, especially not the advertisements. If you are absorbed in reading material, you aren't paying attention. If you absolutely must locate a sleazy personal injury lawyer or astrology hotline, try the Yellow Pages.

2. DON'T LISTEN TO HEADPHONES; if you can't hear what is going on around you, you are more vulnerable and likely not to react quickly.

THE CAMERA hidden in the cigarette pack is passé. These days spies use **HIGH-TECH DEVICES** that are far more miniature. A *cell phone* can harbor a **MICRO CAMERA**. A listening device, complete with tiny **CIRCUIT BOARD**, can be easily *attached to a tie*. For longer ranges, a **SHOTGUN MICROPHONE** that picks up sounds **500 FEET AWAY** can be carried in your *coat pocket.*

3. Don't use your cell phone. Let us count the reasons: YOUR ATTENTION IS DIVERTED.
You make yourself—particularly your phone—a target. And it's incredibly impolite, not to mention uncool.

4. Don't go into an empty train or subway car or sit in a section of the train all by yourself.

5. If you see a problem developing, move away. Don't worry about offending some psychopath. It's no different than being afraid to lock your car doors because you might offend a passing pedestrian.

6. Many commotions, even entertaining ones, are staged to distract you while a confederate picks your bag or pocket. If something unusual starts happening, go into DefCon Level 2.

7. If you see a notice that says BEWARE OF PICK-POCKETS, resist the urge to tap around for your wallet, thus helpfully pinpointing its location for thieves.

8. If someone nearby starts raving, in deep distress from demons within, refrain from responding—just put as much space as you can between you and him. If your compassion gets the best of you, and you feel safe enough to perhaps hand the guy a dollar, you may be whacked from behind by his teammate for your trouble.

● IN HOTELS AND MOTELS

Keeping yourself and your property safe in your hotel room means following one golden rule: never open your door for anybody you don't know, even if she claims to be a hotel employee. First phone the front desk and ask if somebody has been sent to your room, then ask to see staff ID. Even then, don't open the door unless you feel comfortable. Nobody legitimate could possibly begrudge your concern for security.

If you're going out, and there's no safe available in the room or at the front desk, take your valuables with you. That's what a spy would do. A spy would never try to hide something in her room: The opposition either has the room under surveillance or can easily uncover a hiding place.

If you must leave valuables in your room, be creative. Comedian Lenny Bruce had a clever hiding place, as detailed in his biography by Albert Goldman. Bruce had the unfortunate double-whammy of being a drug addict who was under continual surveillance by law-enforcement authorities concerned with the explicit content of his performances. As soon as he arrived in a new hotel room, he would unscrew the plate covering a light switch, hide his stash behind the plate, and then replace the switch cover. Lenny Bruce truly had a spy brain.

In the case of a true emergency, the hotel will evacuate the guests. This could be because of a fire or because of a

terrorist threat, but you never know how long you might be out of your room. Be ready to clear out at a moment's notice. Have casual clothes that are easy to get into, like a sweat suit and athletic shoes, at the ready, as well as your wallet, essential papers, and keys. You don't want to be standing in the lobby or in the freezing cold with the hotel's zebra print robe and black socks. Know the escape routes in the case of a fire, and be prepared to go and stay gone.

WHAT TO DO IF YOU LOSE YOUR ID ON THE ROAD

Losing your identification has never been a pleasant prospect, but in these days of increasing demands for positive ID, it can be a complete nightmare. The good news is, airlines and other carriers are individually responsible for validating identity, so if you can find a sympathetic ear and follow a few basic principles you'll probably be all right—except for those nagging questions of who has your ID and what are they doing with it.

When traveling abroad, you should always carry at least one photocopy of your passport and keep it separate from the real deal. This is the single most crucial move you can make to preserve your sanity (and, in many cases, your vacation).

If you have the facilities to do so, scan your passport and drivers license and email them to yourself before traveling—

that way you can always get at this information even if stripped of every possession. You can then use your passport as a building block for re-creating the rest of your ID.

Losing credit cards is painful but not necessarily costly. Report the loss immediately and your liability will be nil, or at least minimal. Many card issuers will send a replacement lickety split, even to a temporary address.

The best way not to break stride on the road is to separate your IDs and thus minimize your losses. If you have two credit cards, keep one, for example, in a wallet and the other in a bag or money belt with other valuables. Are you doubling your exposure or halving your risk? Erm...yes.

● SURVEILLANCE

● TIPS FOR TAILING

While we are not advocating you go around tailing people—except for that person who keeps skipping out the back door whenever you come home or perhaps to see if your brother-in-law is really going straight out to settle his phone bill with that five hundred bucks you just "loaned" him—it is a good idea to know some of the surveillance methods used by stealthy professionals.

1. Always bring binoculars. The more distance you can put between you and your subject, the lower your odds of being spotted.

2. Change your appearance throughout the course of your surveillance by switching into different caps, sunglasses, and jackets.

3. If you have the luxury of tailing a subject who follows a strict routine over a long period, it's advisable to tail progressively. This involves tailing for a short distance, then dropping back, then starting at the drop-back point the next day and adding more distance to the route, and so on, adding more distance every day. This method greatly lowers the chances of your being spotted, because you are in a different place every day.

4. Top professionals place a tracking device in a subject's car, similar to anti-theft devices such as Lojack. They might also track from miles above, by airplane. If you can afford this level of surveillance, it's likely your subject will never have a clue.

5. If the subject spots you three times, it's over. It's called getting burned.

HOW TO SHAKE A TAIL

Spies are trained to spot or sense surveillance. They're taught to look for patterns around them, such as the same cars or people recurring in different places. Training consists of actually being followed until detection becomes intuitive. You have a certain degree of control if you are aware that you are being tailed.

Unlike in the movies, a real spy does not take immediate evasive action. The sophisticated spy simply goes about her activities, although she may have to abort an operation.

If she's well trained and the mission is vital, she may proceed to carry it out even under surveillance, using such methods as the brush pass, a bump-and-keep-walking technique intended specifically for spies to pass items or documents while under surveillance.

Civilians also come under surveillance through their jobs. For example, an employer might hire a private security firm to investigate inventory shrinkage. If you find you're under surveillance, you should never acknowledge that you know, even if you're innocent. You should also never give the security guys a hard time, because that will only increase the amount of surveillance.

If you're being followed, you might want to take passive steps to elude and confuse the surveillance. A "lite" disguise can make it difficult for someone to describe you or to spot you based on a photo or description. Like spies, security guys do a lot of their work at night, and under cover of darkness a mild disguise can be highly effective.

In a more extreme measure, lone drivers can further confuse surveillance by installing in the passenger seat a "Jack in the Box"—a dummy placed in a car to deceive a tail into thinking there is another person in the car. The Jack in the Box works far better at night. Please note that we do not advocate using this device to gain access to a high-occupancy-vehicle lane. Not even if you give it a name and talk to it.

DRY-CLEANING:
ACTIONS AGENTS TAKE TO DETERMINE IF THEY ARE UNDER SURVEILLANCE AND ELUDE IT

HOW TO CONFIRM YOU ARE BEING TAILED

A harmless tail should be ignored, but what if it's not so benign? If you suspect you are in danger from a tail—perhaps you have the new design for the sports car of the year in your briefcase—you can employ several spy-tried maneuvers to first confirm and then shake the tail.

TWO RIGHT TURNS. The classic counter-surveillance maneuver. Anybody still following you after two right turns is highly suspect, yet you haven't done anything unusual enough to indicate that you are aware of the surveillance.

U-TURN. This maneuver raises the stakes. Anybody following suit and continuing to follow is quite likely a tail.

SIGNAL FOR A RIGHT TURN at an intersection and wait for your suspected tail's right-turn signal to come on. Then go straight through the intersection and see what happens.

ENTER A LEFT-TURN LANE at a traffic light, then change

REMEMBER! THE ENEMY IS WATCHING

JOHN ANTHONY WALKER, the KGB's most important AMERICAN SPY in the 1970s, *betrayed his country* for cold cash. In 1968, the lowly warrant officer walked into the Soviet embassy with a NAVY CODE KEYLIST and sought payment. Thus started a clandestine arrangement of documents dumped by the side of the road in return for grocery BAGS FILLED WITH MONEY. In 1976, Walker retired from the service but not from the lucrative business of PASSING SECRETS. He enlisted his son, brother, and a friend to provide the classified information he sold. In 1984, Walker's ex-wife TURNED THEM IN, but only after the Walker spy ring had supplied an estimated ONE MILLION classified messages to the Soviets—the most shocking spy episode in U.S. NAVAL HISTORY.

your mind after the light turns green and continue traveling straight.

IF YOU'RE ON FOOT, drop a random piece of paper. See if anybody picks it up.

HOW A SPY ESCAPED AMERICAN SURVEILLANCE

In his memoirs, former CIA officer Edward Lee Howard confessed to identifying for the KGB photographs of people with whom he had worked. Some claim his revelations led to the execution of a Soviet scientist who was a CIA mole, as well as the expulsion from Moscow of several American agents and the detention of other Soviets working for the CIA After Howard had been fired from the CIA in 1983, he apparently approached the Soviets and sold out his former colleagues.

He and his wife, Mary, also a former CIA employee, then returned to civilian life—but the CIA caught the scent of Howard's treachery. In September 1985, Howard felt the heat and decided to make his escape. In order to shake his surveillance, he used techniques taught him by the CIA. On what he assumed was a tapped line, he made restaurant reservations, then he and Mary went out to dinner. On the drive home, Mary slowed around a corner and installed a Jack-in-the-Box in the passenger seat while Howard fled into the night. After Mary pulled into their garage, she dialed Edward's dentist, reaching his answering machine. She played a recording of Edward confirming an appointment. Satisfied that the Howards were in for the night, the surveillance team relaxed. Meanwhile, Edward Lee Howard was fleeing the country—becoming the first and only former CIA agent ever to defect to Russia.

PAVEMENT ARTIST: INTELLIGENCE SLANG FOR A TAIL OR STAKEOUT

🔘 IN THE AIR

The world down below looks a lot different from five miles up, and ever since the al Qaeda attacks the world inside the plane is looking a lot different, too. Security experts used to advise total passivity in the event of a terrorist attack. Now the rules of engagement have profoundly changed.

Travel-security expert Dan Mulvenna is a sober, level-headed adviser who always stresses safety over heroics. But even he, in the wake of 9/11, advocates a whatever-it-takes vigilantism if you are truly convinced that a terrorist hijacking is a suicide mission. The following is his advice on what to do if you find yourself on a plane that's been hijacked by what appear to be terrorists.

When they start collecting passports, what should you do?

You've never needed to employ your analytical skills more than now. You have to decide:

- ❑ Are the hijackers collecting passports in order to identify citizens of countries to which they are hostile?
- ❑ If so, are their sentiments such that they are going to be hostile to passengers from my country?
- ❑ Will this hostility manifest itself in my being critically injured or killed?

Conventional spy advice in all dangerous situations is to keep as low a profile as possible. Usually people who stand out from the pack are the ones singled out for punishment. If you fail to turn over your passport, the hijackers may very well take inventory and discover your passport is missing.

On the other hand, if the hijackers begin threatening all citizens of your country, you're better off withholding your passport, even if your excuse to them for not possessing one is as weak as an actress explaining a shoplifting incident as "rehearsing for a role."

How do you know if it's a suicide mission?

If the hijackers make no effort to conceal their faces and names, if their facial expressions are the beautific reflections of a certainty that they will soon be rewarded by their god . . . it doesn't look good.

What do you do if it is a suicide mission?

If you're convinced that the hijackers are on a suicide mission, then go for it. Grab an improvised weapon—a rolled-up magazine, soda can, hot coffee. Even if you've been stripped of your deadly nail clippers at the airport, countless other items commonly found on a commercial flight can enhance your efforts at self-defense.

Which is the safest airline?

The basic principle here is that terrorist hijackings are never simply crimes of opportunity; they are politically motivated. So if your primary concern is not being hijacked, don't look for the airline with the best security; look for the airline least likely to be a target.

By flying with a "target" airline, no matter how airtight their security, you are in essence betting that their security is going to be 100 percent perfect. It's like asking, "Would you rather be shot while wearing a Kevlar vest, or not shot at all?"

Which is the safest seat on an airplane?

Studies of survivors of past air disasters yield no consistent data pointing to the safest seat on an airplane in the case of a crash. In a terrorist incident, though, there is a most desirable place to be seated— in the exit rows above the wings. If your flight has been hijacked, landed, and is sitting on the airport runway, you have the edge over other passengers if you can seize the opportunity to run out onto the wing and escape.

■ ■ ■ ■ THE JAMES WOODS INCIDENT ■ ■ ■ ■

Actor James Woods is best known for his outstanding portrayals of shifty weasels in such films as *Against All Odds, Casino,* and *Citizen Cohn.* Clearly, Woods is a skilled observer of human behavior, particularly of the dubious variety. And this expertise led him to a frightening assessment on a flight from Boston to Los Angeles just one month before the 9/11 al Qaeda attacks.

Woods was concerned about the conduct of four fellow first-class passengers. They appeared to be Middle Eastern, declined food and drink, and made no effort to get comfortable on the six-hour flight. They snubbed the flight attendant, apparently because she was a woman. They engaged in hushed conversation.

In Woods' description, it was as if he'd been onstage at a concert looking out at the audience, and everybody was watching and enjoying the show except four people who were just muttering amongst themselves.

Woods reported his suspicions to the flight crew. Although the journey ended uneventfully, the crew duly filed reports with the FAA. A month later, after the terrorist attacks, Woods was one of tens of thousands to contact his local FBI office and report what he'd observed.

At 6:45 the next morning, two FBI agents showed up at his door. At least two of the men Woods spotted were

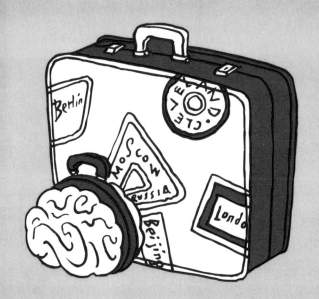

involved in the 9/11 hijackings—Woods' flight had apparently been a rehearsal.

Obviously the authorities cannot take action every time someone voices suspicion about a fellow passenger. But if all travelers were as vigilant as Woods—if everybody developed and used spy-level observation and assessment skills—one wonders whether the terrorists might have been exposed even before boarding their flights.

9

DIGGING THE DIRT

A dozen years ago it would have been difficult to access information we take for granted today. The widespread availability and utility of the Internet has issued in a new era. Today, anyone can log on and amass a spy-worthy dossier before entering into any sensitive interaction.

Still, ye olde-tymey methods are valuable as well. Public records are still more likely to be found in a musty county records building than online. For that reason an assiduous modern spy must be a combination of broadband surfer and vintage gumshoe. In this chapter we'll guide you to the ways that will make you . . . if not totally informed, then how about a little less clueless?

● BASIC DOCUMENTS

YOU CAN ASSEMBLE a detailed portrait of a person's life based on the official documents that formalize landmark life events: birth, death, marriages, court records, property transactions, adoption records, tax filings, police records, and more. Some of these documents are publicly available, some are strictly controlled, and other fall into a gray area—accessible to certain people under certain conditions.

Not long ago, it looked as if all records were going to become available online, with various degrees of accessibility. But with the explosion in identity theft in the past few years, along with other criminal misuses of documents such as stalking, authorities have become spooked at the idea of making everything available to anyone.

> **❝We have slain a large dragon, but we now live in a jungle filled with a bewildering variety of poisonous snakes. And in many ways, the dragon was easier to keep track of.❞**
>
> — CIA DIRECTOR JAMES WOOLSEY, in the wake of the Soviet Union's demise in 1991

FROM FOUR HUNDRED miles up in orbit U.S. satellites can **ZOOM IN** on objects as small as **FOUR INCHES** wide—that's the **SIZE OF A SOFTBALL.**

According to San Francisco-based private investigator Alex Kline, fewer documents are now available online than five years ago. And, he says, that means that people have more privacy. "There's a term called 'practical obscurity,' which means that when records require time and money and hassle to obtain, all that rigmarole, most people won't access those records unless they really need them. But if everything is filed electronically, placed online and made publicly available—not just the index but the actual document—that's a dramatic change."

● WHERE ARE THE RECORDS?

PUBLIC RECORDS IN AMERICA are maintained at the county level, although some states, including California, have begun aggregating all their county records in a single location. There are over 3,000 counties in the U.S. (They're known as "parishes" in Louisiana and "boroughs" in Alaska.) Each county keeps these records at its Department of Vital Statistics.

The availability of these records, including birth, death, and marriage certificates, varies from county to county, and the laws keep changing, generally becoming more restrictive. You have to go down to the building in person, fill out a form, and pay in the range of $10-12 for each record. Increasingly, you also have to demonstrate that you're a relative or have a compelling need for that document. "Because I'm nosy" and "Hey, what am I, suddenly in Communist Russia?" are no longer acceptable reasons.

Court records are kept at the county courthouse. Whenever a person is convicted of a crime, or simply taken into court, a record is created. These records are openly available to the public for a fee, no questions asked.

If someone is arrested and the case never goes to trial, however, then there's no court file. In this case, the arrest record remains internal to the police department that made the arrest. The department can release this information at its discretion, such as to other law-enforcement officials, but it must be mindful of the propriety—and legality—of releasing such information.

In the movies, you might see a police-department employee access an incident report as a favor to another cop, a flirty private investigator, a flirty journalist, even the enraged and vengeful (and flirty) best friend of a recent crime victim. They always say, "I could lose my badge for this," but somehow you know that isn't going to happen. And in earlier days, this actually occurred sometimes. But it's a different world now.

In the old days, police departments had "blind" computer terminals—any officer could anonymously pull up a rap sheet. But today, most departments have tracking systems so that if an officer makes an inquiry, he has to use a password for access. And that leaves a footprint. And so the chances of getting caught have gone way up—cops can lose their jobs and be disgraced for simply "doing a favor."

HOW DO I KNOW WHERE TO LOOK?

This is the tricky part. To begin amassing documents on somebody, you need some toehold of basic information, such as places lived, marital status, or jobs held. If you have nothing, you need to hire someone to start digging, or you need to get digging yourself.

Because so little of this information is available online, if you're in a hurry you might want to take your search to a private investigator (PI). Licensed PI's have entrée to proprietary investigative databases that contain information inaccessible to the general public. For example, they can swiftly pull an address history for the past 20 years or every lawsuit that's ever been filed with a specific named party. A civilian could compile this

CARRIER PIGEONS were used for centuries to carry SECRET MESSAGES because they would return home *in any weather*. Pigeons carried their tiny missives high above ENEMY LINES during both WORLD WARS. Radio communication could be knocked out . . . but not the HOMING PIGEON. Nearly all of the hundreds of thousands of carrier pigeons sent through *enemy fire* COMPLETED THEIR MISSIONS.

information independently, but she would first need to know the name of each county in which a lawsuit was filed, and somehow trace each address individually.

If you have some information to begin with, you can get the ball rolling much more quickly. A person's resume, for example, provides a roadmap to places lived, jobs, education, associations, military records and more. If you're in contact with one person who's known your subject for years, and that person's willing to speak to you in confidence, they should be able to lead you to many of the desired documents.

Given enough time and resources, you can find out pretty much anything about anybody. Even if someone is living "off the grid," seemingly generating no traceable records, a diligent investigator can conduct interviews, dig into the past, find a current residence or trace recent movements. And an arrest record might be part of the mix as well.

■ ■ ■ ■ SPY RESOURCES ■ ■ ■ ■

INTERNATIONAL SPY MUSEUM
www.spymuseum.org
Info on the museum and how to visit, fun facts about spying in general.

THE CIA
www.cia.gov
Welcome to The Company.

THE FBI
www.fbi.gov
Among other things, the website flags "hot" scams.

U.S. DEPARTMENT OF JUSTICE
www.usdoj.gov/criminal/fraud/idtheft.html
This sub-section of the DOJ site features info on identity theft.

FEDERAL TRADE COMMISSION
www.ftc.gov
Info on telemarketing fraud, charity scams, phone swindles, and lottery scams.

IMMIGRATION AND NATURALIZATION SERVICES
www.usdoj.gov
Info on passport fraud and false immigration documents.

PRIVACY RIGHTS CLEARING HOUSE
www.privacyrights.org
Nonprofit organization with tips on how to protect yourself against identity theft, internet fraud, telemarketing, stolen medical records, etc.

■■■■■COLOR-CODED THREAT ALERTS: ■■■■■ LIKE iPOD MINIS, ONLY SCARIER

Your spy instincts have been given a helping hand in assessing the level of danger in the air. The U.S. Office of Homeland Security has obligingly adopted the DefCon (Defense Condition) principle from the military to convey to civilians the gravity of the current situation regarding threats to the public, primarily from terrorism.

There are five **THREAT CONDITIONS**, each identified by a description and corresponding color. From lowest to highest, the levels and colors are:

> **LOW** = Green
> **GUARDED** = Blue
> **ELEVATED** = Yellow
> **HIGH** = Orange
> **SEVERE** = Red

The higher (redder) the **THREAT CONDITION**, the greater the risk of a terrorist attack. This risk includes both the probability of an attack occurring and its potential severity. Threat conditions are assigned by the Attorney

General in consultation with the President's Assistant for Homeland Security.

The guidelines for assessing **THREAT CONDITIONS** look a lot like those for spy-type assessments:

> **1.** To what degree is the threat information **CREDIBLE?**
>
> **2.** To what degree is the threat information **CORROBORATED?**
>
> **3.** To what degree is the threat **SPECIFIC and/or IMMINENT?**
>
> **4. HOW GRAVE** are the potential consequences of the threat?

THREAT CONDITIONS may be assigned for the entire nation, or they may be set for a particular area or affinity group. There are no precise guidelines for assigning different colors—it's more of a "vibe," though no government official would ever call it that, not even that really cool one you see sometimes on the weekends.

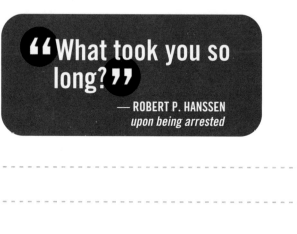

> **"What took you so long?"**
>
> — ROBERT P. HANSSEN
> *upon being arrested*

> **"God gave me both a Brain and a Body."**
> — ROSE O. GREENHOW
> *Confederate spy*

The Handbook of Practical Spying

Text by Jack Barth

Introduction by Peter Earnest,
Executive Director, International Spy Museum

Lisa Lytton, *Editor*
John Paine, *Text Editor*
Pat Daniels, *Text Editor*
Bea Jackson, *Art Director*
Gary Colbert, *Production Director*
Ruthie Thompson, *Design Assistant*
Angie McEvoy, *Additional Research*

With special thanks to Kathleen Coakley, Vice President of
Exhibition Management for the International Spy Museum; Peter Earnest,
Executive Director of the International Spy Museum; and Joan Stanley
of J.G. Stanley & Co., Inc.

Visit the International Spy Museum, Washington, DC and spymuseum.org

One of the world's largest nonprofit scientific and educational organizations,
the National Geographic Society was founded in 1888 "for the increase and diffusion
of geographic knowledge." Fulfilling this mission, the Society educates and inspires
millions every day through its magazines, books, television programs, videos, maps
and atlases, research grants, the National Geographic Bee, teacher workshops, and
innovative classroom materials. The Society is supported through membership dues,
charitable gifts, and income from the sale of its educational products. This support
is vital to National Geographic's mission to increase global understanding and pro-
mote conservation of our planet through exploration, research, and education.

For more information, please call 1-800-NGS LINE (647-5463)
or write to the following address:

National Geographic Society, 1145 17th Street N.W., Washington, D.C. 20036-4688 U.S.A.

Visit the Society's Web site at www.nationalgeographic.com.